Pierre BONNARD

Frontispiece: *After the Shower, 1914. Oil, 37½ x 26". Collection Louis E. Stern, New York.*

JOHN REWALD

Pierre

BONNARD

THE MUSEUM OF MODERN ART

NEW YORK

in collaboration with THE CLEVELAND MUSEUM OF ART

Acknowledgment

On behalf of the Trustees of the Cleveland Museum of Art and the Museum of Modern Art, New York, we wish to express our grateful appreciation of the invaluable collaboration and assistance which we received from Mr. Georges Salles, Director General of the Museums of France, from Mr. Louis Joxe, French Director General of Cultural Relations, and from Mr. René de Messières, Cultural Attaché at the French Embassy. We are particularly grateful to Mr. Charles Terrasse, Curator of the Museum of Fontainebleau, nephew of Bonnard, who acted in Paris as co-director of the retrospective exhibition of the works of Pierre Bonnard upon which this book is based.

We are greatly indebted to Mr. Jean Cassou, Head Curator of the Paris Museum of Modern Art, and to Mr. Bernard Dorival of the same museum, as well as to Messrs. Alphonse Bellier, Jean and Henry Bernheim-Dauberville, Alfred Daber, Marcel Guérin, Albert S. Henraux, Jacques Rodrigues-Henriques, Thadée Natanson and Ari Redon in Paris, Mr. Gustav Zumsteg in Zurich, and Mr. Duncan Macdonald in London, who assisted us with invaluable information. In this country our efforts were supported by Hanna Fund, by Mr. and Mrs. Duncan Phillips, Mr. Sam Salz, Mr. Georges Keller and Mr. Gerstle Mack, who all contributed greatly to the success of this exhibition. Miss Ruth Olson and Mr. Abraham Chanin, of the Museum of Modern Art staff, were most helpful in compiling a list of works by Bonnard now owned in the United States.

We wish to extend our special thanks to all the lenders whose generous collaboration made the exhibition possible.

WILLIAM M. MILLIKEN, *Director*
The Cleveland Museum of Art
MONROE WHEELER, *Director of Exhibitions*
The Museum of Modern Art, New York
JOHN REWALD

Contents

Bonnard in his Studio in Le Cannet, 1944. Photograph by Henri Cartier-Bresson.

Introduction

Pierre Bonnard died on January 23, 1947 in his little house at Le Cannet. He was nearly eighty, and since adolescence had devoted his life to painting. This exhibition, selected from European and American collections, both public and private, attempts to offer a representative selection of his works.

Bonnard's career was extensive, covering more than sixty years and exploring the most diverse territories in art. He treated all manner of subjects, and expressed himself with ease and conviction in every genre. He painted portraits, landscapes, marines and still lifes. He delighted in painting interiors, in depicting village fêtes and scenes of Parisian life. He completed large decorations. He was a lithographer, an etcher, an illustrator of books.

His first professional work was designing posters, at the age of about twenty-two. He lived in Paris for the most part during his early years as a painter, and perhaps no one has expressed better than he the multiple aspects of the city, revealed in their most seductive and characteristic guise. He painted the calm of the side-street, the bustle of the boulevard, the tenderness of a woman's face glimpsed casually, the simplicity of the little shop and the humility of the coach horse, the phantasmagoria of evening lights and sometimes, even, the luxuries of mundane existence. He celebrated, too, the formal beauties and the languors of women, and also domestic scenes and the appealing manners of children. His drawings, lithographs and little canvases were full of a spirit and grace which impressed Renoir.

As soon as he was able — around 1905 — he divided his life into two parts, and though never abandoning the city entirely, spent most of his time in the country, spring and summer in the outskirts of Paris, winter in the Midi. At that point Nature could be felt in his art full-force.

At first he settled in the neighborhood of Saint-Germain-en-Laye, attracted by the warming presence of his friends, Roussel, Vuillard and Maurice Denis. Later he lived not far from Triel and Médan. He settled down finally at Vernon on the edge of the huge Seine valley whose ample and changing horizons charmed him. In the autumn, however, he returned to his family's home in the Dauphiné.

Throughout his life he kept up, in his restless imagination, the search for new vistas and horizons and unfamiliar skies, stopping here and there, always beguiled by an unexpected beauty that he could discover in Auvergne as in Bourgogne, in Provence no less than in Normandie, motivated always by a universal sympathy for beings and things. Easily satisfied, he sometimes used a hotel room as a studio, and would tack a canvas on the wall and begin work, singing. First

9

he would draw in charcoal the basic lines of a composition, working from a quick sketch made in the morning or the day before. Then, little by little, the painting took form — but never quickly. The paintings by Bonnard which are so surprising in their ease and spontaneity, are the fruit of long meditation, of a continuous effort requiring months and sometimes years. He customarily put aside a picture when it was nearly finished. He would take it up again after weeks or months, seeing it with a fresh eye, finding a definitive solution, modifying, accentuating, not fearing even to begin all over again at a still later date. His most lyric works were realized only at the price of long labor.

Before roughly 1895 his palette was extremely clear and his subjects precisely defined — thus revealing his taste for Japanese prints and his regard for the lessons of Gauguin. Afterwards, at Paris, his colors turned gray and sombre. He used blacks, browns and greens, and often enveloped his subjects in halation and mist. But this period was brief. His palette cleared again and its tones grew brighter. Now he tended to dissolve form in particles of light, as the Impressionists had done.

Toward 1915, the anguish of war turned Bonnard inward upon himself. He took stock of his conscience, as Renoir had done before him, and though he was already famous, he went back to school. He immersed himself in the study of form, in problems of composition, as if defying color — "this color," he said, "that bewilders one." And then, feeling himself fully disciplined, he was free again. He burst forth with shattering harmonies of color — purples, shades of orange and violet, yellows. . . .

Needless to say, there can be no question of analyzing in these few lines the evolution of Bonnard, of indicating by precise stages the continuous development of so complex and renewable an artist. He once said himself, without declaiming a preference: "My first pictures were done by instinct, the others with more method perhaps. Instinct which nourishes method can often be superior to a method which nourishes instinct." Still, one should note that Bonnard attained mastery very early, before he was twenty-five.

He has been called the enchanter, the magician, the painter of marvels. He wished to paint only happy things. One will find in his work neither sadness nor suffering, only an occasional trace of melancholy and then merely as an accompaniment to feminine grace.

Bonnard contemplated the world with a vivid and insistent eye, his attention sometimes strangely fugitive, sometimes fixed and absorbed. His was the gaze of the perpetual observer, often mischievous and mildly ironical, but without malice. Tall, slim, a little frail, he remained young and simple to the end of his days, retaining the miraculous youth of the artist and the poet. Affable, kindly, accessible to all, his welcome was unforgettable.

His last painting was *Flowering Almond-tree,* the almond tree of his own garden, thrusting its full white flowers against the blue sky, symbol of spring, an offering to the Nature that was Bonnard's lifelong love.

CHARLES TERRASSE

Pierre
BONNARD

Self Portrait, c. 1925.

The Paris of the Gay Nineties apparently deserves the reputation it enjoys, inasmuch as some of its frolicsome unconcern is reflected even in the artistic life of those years. It would appear that the struggle of young painters was less desperate than it had been before, that their hardships had become more bearable because of a more congenial atmosphere. The discussions of new problems seem to have been untroubled by the burning doubts experienced by previous generations; they were less heated, which is not to say that they were less serious. Ideas simply took shape in a smoother way, they developed more harmoniously without stumbling through the wilderness of uncertainty. And yet it was a period of amazing artistic activity, overflowing with new conceptions, with tendencies that often clashed — but clashed without fury.

Not everybody, however, was gay in those years. Gauguin, embittered by his bad luck, was ready to flee Europe forever. Van Gogh had consumed himself in his eagerness to express his intense sensations; Seurat had set out with solemn determination to reconcile science and art, to be original, as he put it, to "find something new." Cézanne lived in complete retirement in the provinces and Degas became increasingly misanthropic. Nevertheless most of the younger artists grew up in an atmosphere of joyful animation in which the problem of earning a living was alleviated by the general tendency to enjoy life.

It was this Paris which saw Pierre Bonnard become an artist. Born in 1867, shortly before the Franco-Prussian War, he was seventeen when Redon, Seurat and some others founded the *Salon des Indépendants,* nineteen when Seurat exhibited his "Grande Jatte," twenty-three when van Gogh committed suicide. The Eiffel Tower was still new and Queen Victoria already very old. Fashions ran riot with feathers and frills, to the delight of Toulouse-Lautrec, who could be met in all the night-clubs and cabarets. Bonnard was young, receptive, shy, though blessed with a great sense of humor, while Paris, slightly shaken with the strange fever of apprehension that accompanies the turn of a century, decided to eat, drink, and be merry while the going was good.

There could hardly have been a better moment for a young painter to grow up, a more "favorable climate" as Maurice Denis later called it. The Impressionists, no longer forming a solid group, had achieved one of their purposes: they had blown a breach in the dam of bourgeois prejudice. The road seemed open to every boldness. Conscious of this new freedom, the young generation had only to work hard and to dare, in order to show itself worthy of this heritage. It did so eagerly, and began almost immediately to turn against the naturalism of the Impressionists so as to be even freer in its striving for new formulas. An astonishing diversity of tendencies suddenly manifested itself, but seen from a distance they all seem to have integrated themselves logically into the great conquest of a new vision that is at the basis of today's art. In this conquest Bonnard played his part.

Bonnard's background and upbringing were typical of the bourgeois milieu to which his family belonged. His youth was cloudless and uneventful. No decision was made in anger, everything had its time and every problem was solved without hardship. His parents lived in a lovely, somewhat distant suburb of Paris, Fontenay-aux-Roses, where Pierre was born, the second of three children. His father occupied an important post in the War Ministry. He came from the Dauphiné province, at the foot of the Alps, where the family owned an estate and where the Bonnard children usually spent their vacations. At the age of ten Pierre was sent to a boarding school. Later he went to the Lycée de Vanves and subsequently to that of Louis-le-Grand, in the heart of Paris, near the Sorbonne. He specialized in the dead languages and philosophy, passing his baccalaureate examinations without difficulty. His father insisted that he should study law so as to prepare himself for the bar or for government service. Bonnard entered his name without much enthusiasm for his real interest already lay elsewhere, in the life around him which he observed incessantly. And to observe meant to enjoy. Nothing seems ever to have caught his eye that did not fill him with delight. His was the happiest disposition one could imagine.

"I work in the mornings," he wrote to his grandmother, "and in the afternoons I go to the Latin Quarter. It is a long way from the Batignolles district to the Panthéon; fortunately there is the Métro. It amuses me to see the people squashed together, and among them are some pretty faces which I draw in the evenings, from memory, in my sketchbook." [1]

His sketchbook soon meant more to Bonnard than the civil code. Reducing his attendance at the law courses to the absolute minimum, he registered at the Académie Jullian, a private institution where he could draw and paint under rather unobtrusive guidance. His colors were mostly gray and he copied the model conscientiously. He also worked for one year at the Ecole des Beaux-Arts and participated in the Prix de Rome competition, the subject of which was "The Triumph of Mordecai." But the work he submitted was judged "not serious enough" and for all we know this opinion was quite justified. The young Bonnard knew nothing of the stern determination that enabled obedient pupils of the Ecole to climb the ladder of official success. He was unable to submit blindly to academic prejudices and rules. He had no ambition but to express himself freely, to seize the delight that filled his eyes.

Bonnard set out to learn for himself the things a painter ought to know, to seek in the great works of the past the advice he needed. He visited the museums in company with a young artist met at Jullian's, Edouard Vuillard, and together they admired the art of the Orient, especially

Japanese prints. Bonnard sensed in their flat planes, their decorative lines, their asymmetrical compositions a wealth of possibilities. His problem became to find a way to assimilate these elements naturally and without effort, to approach the world around him with Oriental ingenuity and inventiveness. He drew incessantly.

At the Académie Jullian Bonnard found an atmosphere that suited his temperament. He discovered a few young artists who, rising above the doltish majority, were interested in new ideas, ready to embark upon new roads. Besides Edouard Vuillard he soon made friends with other beginners: Maurice Denis, Félix Vallotton, Paul Ranson and Paul Sérusier. It was at Jullian's, in October 1888 — Bonnard was then twenty-one years old — that Sérusier revealed to his friends Gauguin's first attempts at what was later to be called "Symbolism." Sérusier's story *Gauguin* was exciting. From his summer vacation in Brittany, where he had briefly encountered Gauguin, he had brought back a small landscape painted under Gauguin's direction.

"How do you see these trees?" Gauguin had asked. "They are yellow. Well then, put down yellow. And that shadow is rather blue. So render it with pure ultramarine. Those red leaves? Use vermilion."

To his friends Sérusier's small painting looked almost formless because of the extreme degree to which all elements had been synthesized. And Sérusier conveyed to the others Gauguin's "message" that instead of copying nature as one perceived it, one should *represent* it, transmute it into a play of vivid colors, emphasizing simple, expressive, original arabesques for the pleasure of the eyes.

Sérusier explained to them that, according to Gauguin, "the impression of nature must be wedded to the esthetic sentiment which chooses, arranges, simplifies and synthesizes. The painter ought not to rest until he has given birth to the child of his imagination . . . begotten in a union of his mind with reality. . . . Gauguin insisted on a logical construction of composition, on a harmonious apportionment of light and dark colors, the simplification of forms and proportions, so as to endow the outlines of forms with a powerful and eloquent expression. . . . He also insisted upon luminous and pure colors." [2]

"At that time," Gauguin himself later explained to Denis, "I wanted to try everything, to *liberate,* as it were, the young generation." [3] And indeed the new generation was drawn towards him, as one of Bonnard's friends put it, by "the presentiment of a higher reality, a predilection for the mysterious and the unusual, a tendency towards reverie, a mental luxury. . . ." [4]

Sérusier's interpretation of Gauguin's aims was fascinating, but Bonnard tried not to be carried away by his enthusiasm. His was a strange position: he was suddenly being offered a solution to many problems which he had hardly had time to approach, some of which he may have not yet even become aware of. But it would have been too simple just to rally around Gauguin and accept his theories. Could he renounce his healthy curiosity, the joy of experimenting, the thrill of sudden discoveries, by adopting Sérusier's gospel? Could he exchange his enterprising youthfulness for a mature certitude? There was much, certainly, that could be of help in freeing him from the conventions of naturalism, but there was also much that presented the danger of too narrow a formula. Bonnard sensed immediately that the quality of "happy improvisation" which characterized his early efforts was threatened by Gauguin's concepts. He could not permit any cold science to encroach upon his spontaneity; his realism instinctively resisted Sérusier's doctrines.

The endless discussions that followed Sérusier's revelations drew closer together the little group of friends. They began to gather regularly in a small *bistro* near the Académie Jullian. It was Sérusier who called the group the "Nabis" (or rather *Nebiim*) from the Hebrew word for prophets. They were the initiated who found in their beliefs the enthusiasm of the old prophets, bound together by the mystic cords of mutual understanding and the conviction of being closer to the truth than others. To this group belonged the painters Bonnard, Vuillard, Denis, Ibels, Ranson, Piot, Roussel, Séguin, the musician Hermant (in whose house they read Verlaine's poems), the writer Percheron and Denis' friend Lugné-Poë, a young actor. Their chief was Sérusier, seconded by Denis, both well read, absorbed in abstract thought, versed in history and philosophy, always ready to search for definitions, to outline the principles that would help their efforts to progress.

When the others discussed the Primitives, Bonnard thought of Japanese prints, and Ranson, who invented nicknames for his friends, called him *the very Japanese Nabi*. He regularly attended the meetings. The others liked him because, as one of them later said, "prodigiously gifted, but too intelligent to make his superiority felt, he knew how to conceal his brilliant talents under an almost boyish demeanor. Like Vuillard, he loved to work by instinct: with impassioned brush strokes, controlled only remotely by intellect and will. A self-tormenting struggle for advancement was utterly foreign to him. He had a profound aversion for all that in art is merely due to manual dexterity and thus cannot stir emotion." [5]

The discussions of the Nabis covered a wide range of subjects, all related to art. They were, a friend once recalled, "sometimes full of fire expressed in solemn words, not without some tendency towards paradox, and at other moments carried away by unexpected whims." [6] One of the main problems which preoccupied the Nabis is set forth in a letter written in 1889 by Sérusier to Denis: "What part should nature play in a work of art? Where should the line be drawn? And from the standpoint of practical procedure, should one work directly from nature or merely study and remember it? Too much freedom frightens me, poor imitator that I am, and yet my head is filled with so many images evoked by what I see around me at all times that nature seems insignificant and banal." [7]

Whereas Sérusier's dogmatism searched for precise answers, Bonnard listened quietly to the others and was willing to try any system and any technique, not so much because they might lead to *the* truth as because they might yield interesting results. Experimentally inclined, he seemed attracted by new possibilities rather than by the prospect of proving or disproving a theory. This did not prevent him from agreeing with the general ideas of the Nabis. In their discussions, however, Bonnard, fearful of every influence, even his own upon others, always contradicted his friends. To tease Sérusier he even pretended to believe that with the invention of color photography the fate of painting would be sealed.[8]

The Nabis maintained that modeling, the imitation of the third dimension, was not necessary and that a painting should appeal to the beholder not through its subject but through "the ability of its lines and colors to explain themselves." [9] As Denis later put it, the Nabis preferred "expression through decorative quality, through harmony of forms and colors, through the application of pigments, to expression through subject. They believed that for every emotion, for every human thought, there existed a plastic and decorative equivalent, a corresponding beauty." [10]

Denis summed up the result of their discussions in this definition: "It must be remembered that any painting — before being a battle steed, a nude woman, or some anecdote — is essentially a flat surface covered with colors arranged in a certain order." [11]

While the Nabis thus debated the respective merits of traditions and new theories, Gauguin, together with some younger artists who had worked with or under him in Brittany, organized a large exhibition at the Café Volpini during the Paris World's Fair of 1889. For the first time Symbolism (Gauguin then called it "Synthesism") presented itself as a new, collective effort. The public paid little attention but the Nabis found in it, as one of them put it, "one or two simple and obviously true ideas at a moment when we were completely at a loss for guidance."[12] Gauguin's ideas had already germinated in their minds; now they could study for the first time a representative series of his works. In these they discovered remnants of Impressionistic execution combined with simplification of forms, a strange mixture of naïveté and sophistication, of brutality and subtlety, of dogmatism and primitiveness. They may even have found bad taste and grandiose visions. They were startled by the contradictions and stimulated by all that Gauguin had to offer. But only one of the Nabis, only Sérusier, was completely convinced and converted. He told Gauguin: "From now on I am one of yours."

All of the Nabis, in one way or another, subjected themselves to Gauguin's influence. Vuillard and Bonnard, however, were the least affected, possibly because they were less attracted by theories, more concerned with their own sensations, more receptive to the quiet harmonies which they constantly discovered in their daily surroundings. Whereas some of the others, under Gauguin's impact, at first imitated him and only slowly found the way back to themselves — if they found it at all — the two friends never indicated their indebtedness through direct borrowing. Whatever they acquired from Gauguin they assimilated first, and applied it only after it had become thoroughly impregnated with their own spirit. Gauguin helped them to see new things and see them differently; they became aware of possibilities that had theretofore escaped them, but although Gauguin's revelations did enrich their perceptiveness they did not overpower their minds. Thadée Natanson, a schoolfellow of Lugné-Poë's, tells us that the Nabis raised funds to buy one of Gauguin's paintings which each of them was to take home in rotation. Yet several times, when it was Bonnard's turn, he simply forgot or neglected to claim the picture.[13]

A small canvas by Bonnard, representing a dead bird, dated 1889, reveals nothing of Gauguin's influence (*page 60*). It is done in delicate tones, broadly painted, the bird's soft down skillfully detached from the luminous gray background. It might almost have been an early work of Monet though, strangely enough, Bonnard and the Nabis knew as yet little about the Impressionists. The naturalist movement in art was still more familiar to them through the paintings of such vulgarizers as Bastien-Lepage.

For Bonnard the year 1889 was a crucial one, not only because of Gauguin's show. After having failed in his oral law examinations (how could he prepare for them when so many vital things were on his mind?), he had been obliged by his father to enter an administrative service where he felt quite unhappy. But when he succeeded in selling a design for a champagne poster, his father consented to let him become an artist. Having previously lived with his grandmother, Bonnard now rented his first studio, rue Lechapelais, in the Batignolles quarter. That summer he went as usual with his family to Dauphiné. It was there that his brother, then doing his military service, came to spend his furlough accompanied by a young musician, Claude Terrasse. The next year Terrasse married Bonnard's sister, Andrée. A deep friendship was henceforth to unite the painter and the composer.

Bonnard himself must have been called to the service a little later. A painting of a parade, dated 1890, was done while he was living in barracks (*page 61*). It is executed in a flat pattern, opposing blue and red, and introduces into its simplified forms an unmistakable irony. Gauguin's influence is obvious, but how seriously is it taken?

In the fall of 1890 Bonnard was back in Paris, occupying a studio at 28 rue Pigalle. He worked feverishly, not only at paintings and drawings but also at lithographs. It was in this last medium that he tried to combine what he had learned from both the Japanese and Gauguin: flat planes, soft colors, and simplified forms. But he added something entirely his own, a gentle humor that delighted in the unexpected without ever going all the way to caricature. It was as if, while reducing shapes and movements to the utmost, he came close to the grotesque but saved himself from it through a wit that was warm and winning. In his paintings a feeling for harmony, a delicate coloration, softened whatever exaggeration there might have been in composition and design. His projects were manifold: illustrations for sheet music by Terrasse, posters, screens, painted or composed of lithographs, all products that might sell more easily than paintings — which is not to say that he always did sell them.

Bonnard's gay mood contributed not a little to make his studio a rallying center for his friends. Maurice Denis, who lived in the outskirts of Paris in Saint-Germain, appeared there frequently; Vuillard was there practically all the time, and Lugné-Poë as often as possible. When

16

Horse Cab, 1897. Color lithograph for a screen, 7¹¹⁄₁₆ x 17¾". The Museum of Modern Art, New York. Gift of Mrs. John D. Rockefeller, Jr.

Lugné-Poë was called to the army towards the end of 1890, the three friends kept him informed about their lives, though Bonnard was not an easy letter-writer. "I should have sent you news of myself long ago," he admitted, "for I know how much pleasure one derives from a letter during one's first days in the regiment. One needs it to be reminded that one is something more than a registered number and that in the past one's existence was different from that of a beast. Anyway that is how I felt about the army; I was unable to connect my present existence with my former life as a civilian. So, as I said, I should have written to you long ago, but I am torpid and it is only by calling myself the nastiest names that I can force myself to come to a decision.

"Here I am leading a studious and quite exemplary life. . . . I am working on an important picture which is progressing well and which will be exhibited, I hope, at the *Indépendants*. In addition I am planning to do a screen which will also be shown at the exhibition. Otherwise nothing is happening. I may go with Vuillard to see a music publisher, but I do not expect any success as yet in that direction. I have abandoned chromolithography (*ouf!*) for the moment, but I shall take it up again whenever I feel impelled to interrupt my oil painting, in order to vary my pleasures." [14]

And vary his pleasures he did. Whatever he touched he infused with his gentle fantasy. While Vuillard grew grave, intensely searching for the hidden poetry and power of humble objects, while Denis, for the time being, experimented with Seurat's theories and painted in little dots, Bonnard observed the world around him with a twinkling eye. Whatever caught his fancy seemed to reveal, and to him alone, an intimate smile full of tenderness. His paintings of that time, many of them rather small, invariably reflected his delight with the most innocent, the most ordinary, the most inconspicuous things. A delight which he translated without apparent effort

17

into pictorial language, mindful of Denis' definition of a painting as a flat surface covered with colors arranged in a certain order.

When Lugné-Poë, prematurely released from the army, returned in February 1891 to find Denis and Vuillard sharing Bonnard's studio, he unhesitatingly joined them. The studio was, as he himself admitted, "as big as a handkerchief," yet the three painters managed to work there while Lugné-Poë rehearsed his roles and even gave lessons in dramatics. "Bonnard," he wrote later, "was the humorist among us; his nonchalant gaiety, his wit was evident in his pictures, in which a kind of satiric quality was always embodied in the decorative spirit. . . . Bonnard did not resemble Denis or Vuillard in any way, yet all three approached life with a noble determination which was a godsend to me." [15]

Lugné-Poë kept his friends in contact with new ventures in the theatre world which particularly interested Vuillard. He introduced them to Antoine's naturalistic *Théâtre Libre* and spoke of his own dreams of creating something absolutely different by introducing symbolism into the theatre, into sets, costumes, acting and play directing, in an attempt to suggest moods and to impress the audience through indirect means. Maeterlinck and Ibsen absorbed him. He read their works to the painters, as well as verses by Rimbaud and Verlaine and the first writings of a young author of their own generation, André Gide.

The studio in the rue Pigalle saw a host of visitors. Of course the other Nabis, such as Sérusier, Percheron, Ibels and Ranson dropped in frequently. Gauguin himself appeared from time to time, and also a dealer who began to show some interest in the little group, Le Barc de Boutteville. Sérusier introduced a newcomer, the Dutchman Verkade who, under his guidance, became a follower of Gauguin. Lugné-Poë tried to attract some critics and explain to them the works of his friends when these exhibited for the first time in 1891. Bonnard and Denis sent to the *Indépendants;* Vuillard, too timid, preferred to wait. Bonnard showed no less than nine canvases, among them four decorative panels, doubtless for the screen he had been working on. In that same exhibition Seurat was represented by his "Cirque." (A few days after the opening he suddenly died.) Towards the end of that same year the Nabis organized their first group show at the gallery of Le Barc de Boutteville who was thenceforth to handle their work.

As he could not always pay his share of the rent, Lugné-Poë did his bit by selling the works of his friends. He succeeded repeatedly in placing them in the dressing-rooms of famous actors among his acquaintances, such as Coquelin *cadet.* He was not the only one, however, to take an active interest in Bonnard and his comrades. Attracted by Bonnard's champagne poster of 1889, Toulouse-Lautrec (who designed his first poster in 1891) searched out its creator and, enchanted by his and Vuillard's small paintings, tried to find purchasers for them. But Lugné-Poë went even further; having persuaded Maurice Denis to put his theories on paper and having placed his first article, he now took up the pen himself to acquaint the public with the efforts of his friends. He did this on the occasion of a small exhibition of "Impressionists and Symbolists" which they organized in Saint-Germain in the fall of 1891 and in which the participants comprised Denis, Bonnard, Ranson, Sérusier, Verkade; two devotees of pointillism, Gausson and Peduzzi; and this time also Vuillard. Lugné-Poë spoke of their "disdain of vulgar naturalism," of their "love of poetic syntheses." He opposed the concept of art as an imitation of nature with the affirmation that art "really expresses only subjective states and new realities." [16]

1889
Poster
before
TL
1891

France-Champagne, poster, 1891. Color litho-graph, 30¾ x 19¾". The Cleveland Museum of Art.

A more complete definition of the new art, a definition inspired by Gauguin's works, had just been published by Albert Aurier, art critic of the newly founded *Mercure de France.* "The work of art," he wrote, "should be:

1. *Ideological,* because its sole ideal is the expression of the Idea;
2. *Symbolistic,* because it expresses this idea through forms;
3. *Synthetic,* because it presents these forms, these symbols, in such a way that they can be generally understood;
4. *Subjective,* because the object presented is considered not merely as object, but as the symbol of an idea suggested by the subject;
5. And therefore *decorative,* since truly decorative painting as conceived by the Egyptians, and very probably by the Greeks and the Primitives, is nothing but a manifestation of art which is at the same time subjective, synthetic, symbolistic, and ideological."

However, Aurier was careful to add that "the artist who is blessed with all of these talents would be no more than a learned scholar were he not also gifted with *émotivité.*" [17] Indeed, precious as this definition might have appeared to those who had to be convinced of the legitimacy of Symbolism, it is true that no work of art can live through reasoning alone. Can it be surprising then that all Bonnard retained from such scholarly discussions was that *emotivity* alone could help him to harmonize colors and perfect his draftsmanship? [18] He was a mere beginner who had to develop his perceptiveness and his technique before he could attempt to justify his efforts on the basis of theories, if indeed he cared at all to do so.

19

Gauguin meanwhile had left for Tahiti, but his ideas were kept alive by the Nabis, by their discussions, their works, their endeavor to define and propagate the Symbolism to which he had led the way. Having once accepted his leadership, Gauguin's young admirers had begun to construct a theoretical basis for what he had accomplished more or less by instinct; they had broadened the scope of his ideas, had generalized what in the beginning had been an individual attempt to overthrow impressionism. If Symbolism now came slowly into the limelight, it was due to the exertions of Sérusier's group much more than to Gauguin himself. This group found allies among young authors and critics, the Symbolists of literature who were already more firmly established and also better equipped to draw the public's attention to their efforts. By then Verlaine was drinking himself to death and Rimbaud had vanished, but Moréas pompously rolled his words, Mallarmé startled, Charles Morice, Albert Aurier, Julien Leclercq, Félix Fénéon and many others propounded and propagated their principles. In 1891 the Natanson brothers founded the *Revue Blanche,* which from the beginning favored Bonnard, Vuillard and their friends.

The Nabis, no doubt strengthened by the sympathy they had obtained among intellectuals, redoubled their efforts. They "invaded" the theatre, designed sets, made posters, decorated programs, established contact with sculptors (they were joined by Georges Lacombe and by Maillol who, deeply impressed by Gauguin, was then weaving tapestries) , they experimented with projects for furniture, mosaics, stained glass windows and the like. In 1892 Aurier followed up his article on Gauguin with a long study on what had by now become a "movement," a study in which for the first time he reproduced works by the young painters, among them Bonnard.

Aurier's rather obscure syntax may not have reached a wide public, but it helped to define the sources of the Symbolist movement by attempting to prove that this new art followed century-old traditions. His analysis of Symbolism reached back into the past to support his contention that "in nature, every object is, after all, nothing but a symbolized Idea." [19] His arguments and his examples were without doubt suggested by what he had learned from the artists themselves.

Eager to show that theirs was not an isolated effort, Denis and Sérusier had searched not only in the museums but also in contemporary art for expressions of similar tendencies or at least for manifestations that might help them to confound the naturalists. Every venture in this direction seemed a confirmation of their own work. They studied the paintings of Pissarro, who alone among the Impressionists attracted them because he had never cast aside his sense of structure, and those of Seurat who had so vigorously opposed Impressionism. They were torn between the opposite poles of van Gogh's canvases, in which color was so often used as a symbol, and the decorations of Puvis de Chavannes, whose draftsmanship abounded in poetic simplifications. They were interested in the Pre-Raphaelites and their literary sentimentalism on the one hand, and by Cézanne on the other because he had "reduced nature to pictorial elements and eliminated all others."

Denis and Sérusier, Bonnard and Vuillard, Verkade and Roussel went regularly to the little shop of *père* Tanguy where they could study the works of Cézanne, van Gogh, Gauguin and Pissarro. They were among the first and only ones who asked to see the canvases of Cézanne, and their admiration for Tanguy's idols deeply touched the old color merchant. He became their

Left: *Woman with Dog, c. 1892. Watercolor, 10⅛″ x 7¼″. The Springfield Museum of Fine Arts, Springfield, Massachusetts.*
Right: *Family Scene, 1893. Color lithograph, 12⅜ x 7⅛″. Metropolitan Museum of Art, N. Y.*

friend, providing them, as he had done with their forerunners, with paints and other materials, occasionally showing their works in his cramped quarters.

But with only one painter of the older generation did the Nabis establish personal and cordial contact: Odilon Redon. They may have met him through the literary Symbolists who began to show interest in his work. Though already in his fifties, Redon was almost unknown. His sensitive and brooding art had escaped attention or not been understood. It seems natural that his esotericism, his profound originality, his delicate mysticism, his disquieting imagination should have attracted the Symbolist writers. Yet his drawings and lithographs appealed to the Nabis, not so much because they contained literary elements of great beauty and power, as because they displayed the most exquisite handling of black and white; and also because they proclaimed the supremacy of imagination. Gauguin had told them how to grasp the things they saw; Redon, living in a world of strange, sweet and haunting unrealities, knew only how to listen to inner voices. His work was based on inspiration rather than observation, yet there was much that attracted Bonnard and his friends, far though their preoccupations were from Redon's.

The Nabis found Redon a kind and modest man (Gauguin had been neither), quietly

21

devoting himself to the creation of images for which hardly anybody cared. His friendship was paternal, though he always treated them as fellow artists, never with condescension. But the rich experience of his solitary life conferred upon his words and gestures a great authority, coupled with warmth. He was no doctrinaire and abstained from the eager proselytism that was so characteristic of Sérusier. He merely offered his young friends the example of his integrity and the stimulus of his encouragement. They were grateful for both. When, some years later, Maurice Denis painted a "Hommage à Cézanne" in which he assembled Bonnard, Vuillard, Roussel, Sérusier and some others around a still life by Cézanne, he found himself unable to portray Cézanne whom he had never met. It was Redon on whom he focused his composition and his "Hommage à Cézanne" thus became a "Hommage à Redon" as well.

In spite of the friendship that united Redon and Bonnard (Redon drew Bonnard's portrait, Bonnard painted Redon's son) there is no specific trace of Redon's influence on Bonnard's evolution. There seems little doubt, however, that Redon strengthened and deepened Bonnard's interest in lithography — both with and without color — and that Bonnard's prints and illustrations, of which he produced a great number between 1893 and 1900, owe something to the mastery with which Redon expressed himself in this medium. Stylistically, however, Bonnard went his own way.

It seems strange that Bonnard's background in those decisive early years should have been primarily one of Symbolism and mysticism: Denis, deeply religious, drew much of his subject matter from the New Testament (they called him *the Nabi of beautiful icons*). Verkade went even further and became a monk. His friend Filiger devoted himself to meticulous images of Madonnas and saints, inspired by the Italian Primitives. Roussel, attracted by mythology, was influenced by Puvis de Chavannes. Sérusier confined himself to Gauguin's Symbolism. Redon reached for the supernatural. Only Vuillard and Bonnard maintained a firm contact with the world of every day. Yet, for the time being, they cast their impressions into decorative patterns that asserted their kinship with the Nabis.

In 1892 most of the Nabis exhibited again at the *Indépendants* where Bonnard showed seven canvases; they also organized another group exhibition in the small gallery of Le Barc de Boutteville. In the fall of that same year they exhibited once more in Saint-Germain — Bonnard and Vuillard among them — and the critic Roger Marx, who had already commented favorably upon their efforts, wrote: "We shall never grow weary of repeating how much decorative art is entitled to expect from artists who, in their compositions, pay more attention than has ever been paid before to the rhythm of a line, the quality of an arabesque, to alternations of calm and movement, of voids and filled spaces." [20]

Gauguin's influence slowly began to vanish and Maurice Denis later remembered that "at the exhibitions of Le Barc de Boutteville, since the end of 1891, the areas of flat colors no longer appeared with such insistence, the forms were no longer set within black outlines, the exclusive use of pure color was no more." Denis attributed this evolution partly to the absence of Gauguin and partly to an inclination of some Nabis "towards more sentimental experiments and more refined processes." [21] It may not be wrong to visualize Bonnard and Vuillard as the originators of these "sentimental experiments," these "refined processes."

Hailing their promising contact with the dealer Le Barc de Boutteville, Maurice Denis now

Dogs, 1893. Lithograph, 14⁷/₁₆ x 10¼". The Museum of Modern Art, New York. Gift of Mrs. John D. Rockefeller, Jr.

drew public attention to the ways in which the decorative abilities of his friends might be practically exploited: "One of the exhibitors might do fanciful and attractive posters. Another could make wallpapers of imaginative design, very modern tapestries and furniture of unusual style. A third might possibly produce sombre mosaics or dazzling stained glass windows. Where is the industrialist who would willingly avail himself of the valuable collaboration of these decorators, so as to consume a little of the time they devote to the execution of far too many paintings?" [22]

No industrialist took the hint, but Lugné-Poë was soon to find a way to keep his friends from painting too many pictures: he commissioned them to do stage sets for the *Théâtre d'Art,* his first venture as an independent director, in which he was associated with the poet Paul Fort. Thus in 1892 the painters designed for him a series of sets and costumes. Roger Marx, impressed by their achievements, immediately praised the theatrical scenery of Sérusier, Ranson, Denis, Bonnard and Vuillard (Bonnard had done his for a play called "Fièrabras," and Vuillard's subject had been "Berthe aux grands piés"). But the real impulse came in the fall of 1893, when Lugné-Poë founded his *Théâtre de l'Oeuvre,* for which he rented the Bouffes-du-Nord, and began to rehearse an Ibsen drama.

In his *Souvenirs* Lugné-Poë tells that Vuillard, assisted by Bonnard, Ranson and Sérusier, "agreed to work on the cold floor of the scenery storehouse in the rue de la Chapelle. . . . How did our good friends escape death from bronchitis? It must be admitted that Vuillard and his companions, repainting at seven or eight in the morning the old flats we had picked up, risked their health and their youth in the undertaking. This scenery storehouse of the Bouffes-du-Nord, without a roof, was exposed to every wind and had no heating system of any kind. . . ." [23] Yet the friends went to work with enthusiasm and also made lithographs for the various theatre programs, a task for which Lugné-Poë secured the collaboration of some non-Nabis, including Lautrec.

According to the description of a contemporary, the Nabis, for their sets, employed "simplified design, use of only those elements indispensable to the creation of each scene, stylization, complete harmony of décor and costume," and avoided all *trompe l'oeil*.[24]

It looked as if Bonnard had found his niche among the "decorators," as if his ingenuity, his feeling for ornament, his partiality for effective arrangements were to confine him to a definite and limited field of expression. But the truth is that he slowly tried to go beyond them. Neither Gauguin's return from Tahiti in 1893 nor a large showing of prints by Utamaro and Hiroshige could deflect him from his course. When he sent his work for the third time to the *Indépendants* in 1893, and also to Le Barc de Boutteville, Roger Marx discovered in his paintings more than pleasing arrangements of color and line. "His complete success can no longer be doubted," he wrote. "His is one of the most spontaneous, most strikingly original temperaments. . . . M. Bonnard catches instantaneous poses, he pounces upon unconscious gestures, he captures the most fleeting expressions; he is gifted with the ability to select and quickly absorb the pictorial elements in any scene, and in support of this gift he is able to draw upon a delicate sense of humor, sometimes ironic, always very French." [25]

Although he was surrounded by comrades haunted by ideas which they endeavored to translate into a language of ornament, Bonnard received his creative impulse from visual experience alone. In some of his earlier works he had been anxious to fit his sensations into the austere frame of sinuous contours, but his spontaneity little by little gained the upper hand. The preoccupation with "style" advocated by Gauguin could lead to just that and nothing more. Did it not, in fact, lead eventually to Art Nouveau with its mannerisms and often hollow performances? Style threatened to become a prison for his perceptions, and Bonnard understood, as Sérusier did not, that style is not an end in itself.

It was possibly for this reason that Bonnard so greatly admired Degas and Lautrec. They had achieved personal style not for its own sake but as a result of their efforts to cast their observations into pertinent forms. They had done what *he* wanted to do, observed intently and based their art upon what they saw. They had developed draftsmanship not according to preconceived ideas but through the will to grasp the essential aspects of their subjects. This will had helped

The Fair, c. 1898. Oil on cardboard, 13¾ x 10⅝". Private collection, Paris.

them to achieve appropriate means of expression. To them, line was a living element and not a mental product like Gauguin's, nor were their colors arbitrary like his. Their imaginations did not interfere with their conceptions of precision, but rather helped them to present their subjects from new angles and to obtain more striking compositions. Though the range of these subjects was more or less limited, their approach to and treatment of their subjects must have encouraged Bonnard to turn his back on Symbolism and focus his attention on what he had always loved, his surroundings.

Thus Bonnard set out to capture in his work what no other painter of his time had observed: the little incidents of Parisian life, the things of which nobody seems to be aware because they repeat themselves continually and constitute in their endless repetition the common elements of daily life. It took the eye of a poetic explorer to be attracted by what everybody saw and eventually even ceased to see because it was neither new nor unusual. Pissarro was beginning to paint the boulevards, the Seine quais and the bridges, seen through his windows, but Bonnard descended into the streets and the squares, watching with equal interest people, horses, dogs and trees.

If there exists such a thing as the exquisiteness of banality, that was exactly what Bonnard discovered. Or would it be more correct to say that nothing is banal in itself but that it takes an artist like Bonnard to make us conscious of the wasted charm which surrounds us? His sensibilities were stirred by the awkward grace of a girl carrying a laundry basket through an empty street, by the tired look of a cab-horse on a busy boulevard, by the patter of children's feet hurry-

Houses on a Court, 1895. Color lithograph, 13¹³⁄₁₆ x 10¼″. The Metropolitan Museum of Art, New York.

ing to school, by reddened faces under umbrellas in a snowdrift, by dogs assembling at street corners, by people browsing before an antique shop, by the characteristic movements of women bustling across a street. Cobblestones and monotonous façades, huddled roofs and old walls contributed their delicate coloration, their hidden poetry; broad avenues, busy street vendors, cafés on sidewalks offered him their intricate patterns, their noisy agitation.

It was not by mere chance that Bonnard's first portfolio of lithographs in color presented "Quelques aspects de la vie de Paris." It was published in 1895 by Ambroise Vollard, who had just opened a gallery in the rue Laffitte. These lithographs seem almost improvised, with their nervous web of lines and hatchings, their large flat areas or cottony scrawls, their uncommon browns, grays and violets, yet they are actually marvels of precise observation and complete mastery of technical means. As an example of Bonnard's precision, Vollard reports that a friend of his recognized his wife and daughter in one of the street scenes.[26]

Bonnard exhibited these lithographs and some drawings at Vollard's, together with prints and drawings by Lautrec. And in that same year of 1895 the works of the two artists were again neighbors at the official Salon, where Tiffany of New York (the only one to heed Denis' advice to industrialists) showed a series of stained glass windows executed after designs not only by Bonnard and Lautrec but also by Roussel, Vuillard, Ibels, Sérusier, Denis and others. Lautrec began to find himself frequently in the company of the Nabis and particularly in that of Bonnard.

26

Bridge, 1895. Color lithograph, 10⅝ x 16⅛". The Metropolitan Museum of Art, New York.

Their genuine friendship and admiration for each other's talent, however, are not reflected in their works, though some of Lautrec's stylistic influence may be detected in Bonnard's lithographs. Occasionally Bonnard ventured into Lautrec's "own" domain of Parisian night life: Montmartre, Boulevard Clichy, Place Blanche, Place Pigalle.

No record of Paris during the Gay Nineties could be complete without a study of its aspects after nightfall. To some its real life unfolded only then, and it is not surprising that Bonnard should have been attracted by the gaslit streets, the fairs, the cafés. But while Lautrec observed this night life from the viewpoint of a participant in the merriment, intimately familiar with its psychology, Bonnard seems to have remained on the outside, a silent witness. He watched the goings-on not with Lautrec's acid sharpness but with the amused eye of a child fascinated by an unsuspected world. It even appears that the circus enchanted him more than the cabarets. There was always a childlike gaiety in his approach, as if he discovered for the first time something completely new; and in a way that was exactly what he did. In later years he was to stress the "importance of an unexpected impression," [27] but to a certain extent everything seemed unexpected to him because he always anticipated new visual adventures, because he never tired of exploring his surroundings with the excitement of a seafarer who sets foot on *terra incognita*. What made his works of that period so appealing was the naïveté of his wonderment at the things he saw, coupled with the somewhat sophisticated delicacy with which he retained them.

27

Vegetable Vendor, 1895. Color lithograph, 11⅞₁₆ x 13⅜". The Metropolitan Museum of Art, New York.

His colors were often dark or at least low-keyed. He frequently used black. He favored blues, soft grays, smoky yellows, but he always introduced into such sober color schemes some accent, vivid or subtle, some fresh note, vibrant and gay, around which the entire composition seemed to revolve. These accents, apparently put there in obedience to a sudden whim, testify to the brilliant sureness of his taste. As often as not they consist of warm colors which enliven cold tonalities. Sometimes a similar accent also brings warmth to the subject itself: a view of roofs and chimneys receives life and joy from a tiny birdcage on a window ledge *(page 67)*.

The reduced color scheme that characterizes Bonnard's paintings of the middle nineties has been interpreted as a reflection of his lithographic work, for which he had to content himself with a range of a few colors only. Yet this relationship seems a rather superficial one. Indeed, in his prints Bonnard achieved a truly amazing variety of nuances, and never appears to have been embarrassed by the limitations of his medium. In his paintings, on the other hand, he intentionally restricted himself so as to enhance the unexpected quality of a bright spot. André Mellerio, one of the first to appreciate Bonnard's lithographs, actually went so far as to say that "the subdued effects he frequently sought in his oils prepared him" for the execution of color prints.[28]

The Nursery, c. 1897. Pen and ink, 6½ x 4½". Collection Marcel Guiot, Paris.

Bonnard often renounced color altogether and covered page after page of his sketchbooks with quick notations made in pen and ink or with the brush. It was in these brush drawings particularly that he attained a freshness and mastery comparable only to the sureness of strokes, the inventive placing, the summary characterization achieved by the Chinese and Japanese. He infused his spots and lines, his dots and strokes with so much wit, so much tenderness, so much simplicity that these unpretentious sketches deserve special attention among his output of those years. They are buried, unfortunately, in old issues of the *Revue Blanche* whose pages he crowded with these small gems in black and white. Some of them appeared again in the first book illustrated by him, Peter Nansen's *Marie,* published by the same periodical.

Besides these sketches, prints and views of Paris there was another subject dear to Bonnard's heart: interiors with family scenes. Here his interests coincided with those of Vuillard, whose entire attention seems to have been focused upon his mother's dressmaking workroom and the quiet world enclosed by the walls of his home. Unlike his bachelor friend, however, Bonnard was a family man into whose life Marthe, his wife, and the small Terrasse children brought new opportunities for tender observation, which he also extended to his pets: dogs and cats by which he always seems to have been surrounded and which he painted or rather portrayed with the same love as his sister's babies. In the nursery and in the peaceful comfort of French middle-class dining-rooms he found still lifes of food, wallpapers whose flowers vied with gaily checked dresses, children and animals around the dinner table, nurslings in their mothers' arms. Insensitive to what has been called the "hierarchy" of objects, he observed them all with the same warmth and delight, treated them as what they were to him: pictorial elements the importance of which depended upon their color and form, their place in his composition. But he did not go so far as Vuillard sometimes did in almost abolishing the individual life of objects and beings, reducing them to mere patterns in a mosaic.

The difference between Bonnard and Vuillard was concisely analyzed by Gustave Geffroy when Bonnard organized his first one-man show in January 1896, at Durand-Ruel's. He was then twenty-eight years old and ready to set before the public the results of his efforts during the last five years. He exhibited forty-nine paintings and although these are not dated in the catalog, it seems that the artist did not include any works prior to 1891, the year in which he had begun to shake off the impact of Gauguin. He also showed two posters, a screen, some lithographs and his illustrations for Terrasse's *Solfège*. There were portraits, street scenes, interiors, studies of children and animals, and circus scenes, but few still lifes, landscapes or nudes. Several paintings were lent by Thadée Natanson, one of the first to collect Bonnard's work.

In his review Geffroy, a childhood friend of Lugné-Poë's, commented: "Vuillard is a clearer and more vivid colorist, more boldly bursting forth into rich patterns of blue, red, golden yellow; and at the same time one feels that his spirit is melancholy, his thoughts are grave. Bonnard, on the other hand, is a gray painter, fond of purplish, russet, somber tones; and yet in every stroke his shrewd observation, his impish gaiety, are revealed with charming distinction. . . . A curious line in movement, of a monkeylike suppleness, captures these casual gestures of the streets, these fleeting expressions born and vanished in an instant. It is the poetry of a life that is past, the remembrance of things, of animals, of human beings. The amused regard of the artist shifts from city to country, and thus is created, delicately, unerringly, a work full of promise, ingenuous and thoughtful, in touch with real life." [29]

But not everybody shared this view. Resentful of Bonnard's Symbolistic beginnings, unconvinced by his attempt to harmonize his instinctive feeling for decorative effects with the realism of his observation, and possibly irritated by the opaque and often dark colors which he relished, the old Impressionists condemned his work in no uncertain terms. Wrote Camille Pissarro to his eldest son: "Another Symbolist has failed miserably! And one whose coming triumph was hailed by Geffroy in *Le Journal*. All the painters worth anything, Puvis, Degas, Renoir, Monet and your humble servant, unanimously term hideous the exhibition held at Durand-Ruel's of the Symbolist named Bonnard. Moreover, the show was a complete fiasco." [30] (It is known that Pissarro, Degas, Renoir and Monet later revised their judgment.)

Was the exhibition really such a failure? There is nothing to indicate it; nor, on the other hand, is there anything to disprove Pissarro's contention, except the undiminished gaiety and apparent unconcern with which Bonnard pursued his work. If he ever went hungry, he certainly took good care not to let anybody know. His modesty would not allow him to act the martyr, partly because he did not consider that his own fate mattered much, and partly because he did not think of his art in such dramatic terms as did, for instance, Gauguin. By simply not sub-

Left: *Laundry Girl, 1896. Color lithograph, 11⁷⁄₁₆ x 7⅞". The Brooklyn Museum, New York.*
Right: *Album Cover, 1895. Lithograph, 15¹¹⁄₁₆ x 11⅜". Private collection, New York.*

mitting anything to the Salon, Bonnard avoided becoming a victim of the blindness proverbially manifested by all French Salon juries; he sent his work instead to the jury-free *Indépendants*. He never sought to "impose" himself or merely to attract attention, and he never showed any signs of frustration when his efforts went unnoticed. If he cared little for success, his wife cared even less. Quiet and almost pathologically shy, though fond of loud colors, Martha Bonnard intensely disliked and shrank from social contacts.

About Bonnard's financial situation in those days nothing is known, but he was always so modest in his needs, so unconcerned with comfort, that he was satisfied with very little. Vollard, since he had taken an interest in the group, tried to sell Bonnard's works, but he tells in his recollections that only Denis' canvases sold readily. Though primarily a picture dealer, Vollard was then gradually becoming "one of the most ardent and active devotees of the publication of prints."[31] His first venture in this field had been Bonnard's portfolio of Paris views in 1895. In 1896 and again in 1897 he published an Album of Painter-Engravers, each containing prints by various artists more or less indiscriminately assembled. Bonnard was represented in both Albums. In 1897 Vollard also conceived the idea of publishing a book by Verlaine with illustrations and his choice fell once more upon Bonnard, of whom Mellerio wrote in those days that he showed in his lithographs a "refined conception as well as simple craftsmanship, tending

Ne fronce plus ces sourcils-ci,
Casta, ni cette bouche-ci,
Laisse-moi puiser tous tes baumes,
Piana, sucrés, salés, poivrés,
Et laisse-moi boire, poivrés,
Salés, sucrés, tes sacrés baumes.

Page from Parallèlement, 1900. Lithograph, 11¾ x 9½". The Spencer Collection, The New York Public Library.

to produce a delicate harmony, concise and very expressive drawing, together with a quality of airy grace." [32]

The project of illustrating a book with lithographs instead of the customary woodcuts was quite a novel one, at least in so far as the illustrations were not to appear on separate pages but were to be intermingled with the text. Vollard chose Verlaine's *Parallèlement* and gave Bonnard free rein. The choice of both book and illustrator was extremely happy. Bonnard surrounded the verses with delicate sketches, delightful, fanciful drawings, which overflowed the margins, insinuated themselves between the lines and filled the pages of the book with their whimsical charm. His lithographs were printed in either rose or blue, thus adding a touch of color and also of lusciousness, a gay fluttering of sensuous accompaniments to Verlaine's poems, capturing their erotic mood. (Some of the same spirit also appears in Bonnard's paintings of nudes done at that period.)

Highly satisfied with Bonnard's illustrations, Vollard shortly afterwards commissioned the artist to supply a set of lithographs for *Daphnis et Chloé*. This time Bonnard adopted a dif-

Illustration for Daphnis et Chloé, 1902.
*Lithograph, 5⅞ x 5½″. The Museum
of Modern Art, New York. Gift of Mrs.
John D. Rockefeller, Jr.*

ferent mode of presentation. The text and the illustrations are clearly separated; each page is divided, the upper two-thirds containing the lithograph in rectangular format, while several lines of text fill the lower part of the page. The illustrations have the freshness of sketches cast lightly on the paper, but since they are arranged with absolute regularity, they have nothing of the improvised aspect that distinguishes his first volume. Far from encumbering the text, they are like mirrors in which are reflected the fields and the herds, the trees and the streams, the flowers and the two lovers celebrated by Longus.

But Vollard paid little for these commissions, and it is true that he did not always find it easy to sell his publications, so very unlike the popular illustrated books with their almost photographic images repeating literally the episodes of the text. Bonnard's chief recompense for his work was the pleasure of executing projects entirely to his own liking, that appealed to his decorative sense as well as to his passionate draftsmanship. Therefore when, in 1898 or 1899, the Bernheim-Jeunes offered to enter into an agreement with him, Bonnard promised to let them have thenceforth the first choice among his paintings. He had met these dealers through Vallotton who had married into their family; owing to their efforts Bonnard was to reach a steadily growing public. He was too honest and faithful to break his pledge, but he was at the same time too independent to enter into a formal contract which would have allotted to the Bernheims the totality of his work. The Bernheims thus handled most of Bonnard's work for some forty years and assured him of a regular and slowly rising income.

Whether or not he found it easy to earn his living, it is certain that Bonnard was happy in his work and happy also in the small circle of his devoted friends and admirers. It comprised mainly the comrades of his early years; Bonnard was extremely faithful in his affections and attachments, and at the same time very slow to make new friends, very reluctant to admit anyone to intimacy. The Nabis and those with whom Bonnard had exhibited at Le Barc de Boutteville's or at the *Indépendants* now gathered in Vollard's famous cellar beneath his gallery, where Bonnard sometimes caught glimpses of his elders, Pissarro, Degas, Renoir. Nearby were the offices of the *Revue Blanche*. Its contributors formed a group centered around Thadée Natanson, who never tired of proclaiming his affectionate admiration for Bonnard as well as for Lautrec. Other painters favored by Natanson were Vuillard, Roussel and Vallotton. All of them contributed illustrations and original lithographs to the review. They were frequently called "the painters of the *Revue Blanche*." Bonnard also designed a poster and the covers for an album of prints for the periodical.

The *Revue Blanche* became one of the poles of Bonnard's life; through it he maintained an active contact with the literary movements of the time. He liked to come to the office about five in the afternoon when authors and artists assembled for animated exchanges of views. Occasionally Bonnard and Vuillard exhibited recent works in this office, at 1 rue Laffitte.

The *Revue Blanche* then occupied an important position in French literary life, owing to the fact that it was not tied up with any of the opposing factions of Symbolism and Naturalism (an attitude not unlike Bonnard's own). Denying that these antagonists monopolized the truth, the *Revue Blanche* published anything of interest and of quality, whatever its source. Its formula appealed to all who were tired of the internal quarrels of literary cliques. In the art field, too, it showed a great eclecticism. The review published Gauguin's *Noa-Noa*, Signac's *D'Eugène Delacroix au Néo-Impressionnisme* as well as an extremely reactionary article by Tolstoy on *Les Décadents* in which he attacked the Impressionists, Symbolists and the whole modern literary movement in France. Nor was the *Revue Blanche* committed politically, although during the Dreyfus trial its editors, contributors and friends collectively took a firm stand in favor of the innocent captain.

Among the contributors of the *Revue Blanche* were Proust, Verlaine and Mallarmé, Maeterlinck, Romain Coolus (a friend of Lautrec's), Verhaeren, Jules Renard, and Monet's panegyrist Octave Mirbeau who showed a great liking for Bonnard's work. There were also Gide, Léon Blum, Claudel, Péguy, Debussy and scores of others, among them Alfred Jarry. But Bonnard struck up a special friendship with the secretary of the review, the strange Félix Fénéon, who paid homage to the painter with silent devotion.

When, in 1896, Claude Terrasse settled in Paris, his brother-in-law introduced him to this circle of friends and thus established the contact between Jarry and Terrasse which was to lead to their collaboration at the *Théâtre des Pantins* on Jarry's *Ubu Roi*. Bonnard helped to execute the marionettes from Jarry's sketches, Terrasse wrote the music, Jarry supplied the controversial and provocative text. In December 1896 the play was presented — this time with live actors — at Lugné-Poë's *Théâtre de l'Oeuvre;* the sets were the collective work of Bonnard, Vuillard, Lautrec, Sérusier and Ranson. The play was greeted with jeers and protests.

Marionettes seem to have fascinated Bonnard and his friends.[33] In 1892-93 Ranson had already organized presentations of Maeterlinck's *Les sept Princesses.* Later he presented in his home little comedies written by himself, with marionettes made by Lacombe and music by Terrasse. And in 1898 the *Théâtre des Pantins* privately presented to a small audience of guests Franc-Nohain's *Vive la France,* prohibited by the censor. The music was once more by Terrasse, the marionettes were modeled by Bonnard.[34] Bonnard also drew the covers for a set of sheet music published by the *Mercure de France* for the *Théâtre des Pantins*: verses by Franc-Nohain, music by Terrasse.

Bonnard was so busy that winter of 1896-97, probably on account of Terrasse's arrival, that he neglected to send anything to the exhibition of *La Libre Esthétique* in Brussels, to which he had been invited, and this in spite of the fact that he had accepted the invitation. Nor did Vuillard exhibit anything. And even the following year Bonnard sent to Brussels nothing but some lithographs, though he must have known that *La Libre Esthétique* was then the most active center of *avant-garde art,* more active certainly than any French group of painters and more concerned with propagating the work of the new generation.

By now the Nabis were no longer anything more than a loose association of friends who had all reached their thirties and were going their own ways. Their friendship had been based not on a common belief in doctrines, but on the similarity of their aspirations and mutual respect for each other's individuality. Thus they were able to develop in various directions without having to sever connections between themselves. But the fact remains that they slowly grew apart. This became particularly clear when Sérusier returned in 1897 from a short visit to Prague where he had elaborated a new esthetic with Verkade, a new hieratism, based on mathematics, on numbers, on geometry, on what he called the "holy measures." While Denis and Ranson showed great interest in his new theories, Sérusier reported to Verkade with some resignation that Bonnard, Vuillard and Roussel had remained indifferent. They were in no way attracted by his system and measurements; it was with regret that Sérusier saw them confine themselves to what he called disdainfully their "individual sensibility."[35] Within the former circle of friends Bonnard, Vuillard and Roussel, who had married Vuillard's sister, now constituted a small group of their own.

The Nabis exhibited once more as a group, or at least grouped themselves together, in 1899, when André Mellerio organized an exhibition at Durand-Ruel's which aimed to "assemble all contemporary trends." Each trend was represented by a group of artists, among whom the Nabis and their friends constituted by far the most numerous contingent. Then there were Signac and the other followers of Seurat, a small group of adherents of the Impressionists, and also some of Gauguin's more "faithful" disciples. Only one artist was listed altogether by himself: Odilon Redon. If it was a tribute to his unique genius that he belonged to no group and had no followers, it would be wrong to think that he was isolated. In a way the whole exhibition revolved around him, and ties of friendship and admiration attached practically all of the younger artists to him. Bonnard, in any event, continued to go frequently to Redon's home, if not to ask for advice, at least to obtain his opinion.

Bonnard was represented by twelve paintings at the Durand-Ruel show. Geffroy once more praised his work: "There is a clownish grace, a catlike agility, in his figures of children and women, in his landscapes, all painted with an apparent negligence, a kind of disorder, which soon reveals the very delightful spirit of a painter who can harmonize." [36] But the influential critic of *Le Temps* thought otherwise: "Bonnard has gained some firmness, yet his compositions always have some traces of caricature, his interiors lack air, and his color is distinguished only by modulations which are skillful enough but exceedingly monotonous in the blacks." [37]

It was at this exhibition, however, that Camille Pissarro revised his first impression and told one of his sons: "This young artist will go far, for he has a painter's eye."

About 1900 Bonnard's work underwent a marked change. He began to experiment with a rich, opaque impasto, with modeling and vivid brushwork. Although his colors did not become exactly bright, at least there appeared in his paintings blues and greens of greater intensity, and also often white. Backgrounds which before had frequently been used primarily to offset the central theme of his canvases, now began to be crowded with details and thus to participate more actively in the composition. Portraits were no longer set against neutral backgrounds; instead the models were surrounded by familiar objects as, for instance, in the likeness of Claude Terrasse, who is represented in a setting consisting of his piano, sheet music, books, paintings on the wall, as well as two of his children. Bonnard's subjects not only gained greater plasticity, they also came closer to life, environed as they were by a host of details lovingly observed. Yet there was no dryness in the painter's presentation of many secondary objects; his awareness of their presence merely testified to his desire to go beyond the enchantment of first impressions, to penetrate his subjects more thoroughly, to widen the scope of his pictorial problems.

If Bonnard now shunned simplifications, he still showed, as in his earlier works, some of that impish gaiety which endeared him to his friends. The details that cluttered up his compositions frequently provided a note of warmth if not of humor. There was hardly a still life, a landscape, or interior into which he did not introduce, at least in a small corner, the profile of his basset-hound or the figure of a cat, and sometimes also the head of his wife. Their presence adds life, often quite unexpectedly, in particular to what in Bonnard's mother tongue is called a *nature morte*. He seemed to relish small incidents of innocent charm — "Bonnard loves the accidental," Degas has said. In one of his most important works of that period, the "Bourgeois Afternoon," a large canvas in which Bonnard assembled various members of his family on the lawn before their house in Dauphiné, Grand-Lemps, there appears as much irony as tenderness in the characterization of adults and children; and the animals too, especially the cat with its kitten, are treated with the chuckle of a smiling story-teller. There is indeed a narrative quality in these paintings,

Bourgeois Afternoon (the Terrasse family), 1902-03. Oil, 54¾ x 83½". Private collection Bernheim-Jeune, Paris.

in which Bonnard's good-natured humor expresses itself with greater directness than before. "It's like a little fable by La Fontaine," Vuillard once told Signac in front of one of his friend's pictures.[38]

The "Bourgeois Afternoon" was exhibited in 1903 at the newly founded *Salon d'Automne*. When Bonnard showed there again, two years later, André Gide commented on his work: "How explain to those who are not sensitive to them the interest of M. Bonnard's canvases? *Esprit,* frolic even, rather than reason make of each of them something strangely new and exciting. Investigation, analysis do not exhaust the kind of esthetic amusement which one savors in front of them, because it springs from the color itself, from the drawing, and not from some explainable ingeniousness. Whether he paints an omnibus, a dog, a cat, a stool, his very touch is mischievous, quite independent of the subject." [39]

It was possibly Bonnard's sense of the comical — too mild to be called a sense of the grotesque — that led him to say that "the unlikely is very often the real truth." [27] He thus did not hesitate to shorten arms or legs, sometimes almost to eliminate the bone structure of his models. In his "Bourgeois Afternoon" a pose such as that of Claude Terrasse, at the left, through its disregard for anatomical exactness, conveys precisely the relaxed attitude that had struck the painter. This freedom is still more evident in many of Bonnard's nudes, which he began to paint in increasing number. His models never actually "posed," he preferred to watch them while they washed or dressed, or even simply while they rested. Though intimately familiar with their movements, he frequently depicted attitudes which, in their improbability, express the feline character that is common to all the nudes he painted. These attitudes seem merely "suggested" by the model, and represent not what the painter actually saw at a given moment, but rather the sum total of his observations from nature.

Degas, in his studies of nudes — and in those of dancers as well — often shows an arrested movement which reflects the one just completed and foretells the one about to follow. He achieved this by representing his models in suspended motion, in the correct attitude of a single instant, caught with precision and cast upon paper or canvas with such unerring instinct that it remains alive as a fleeting second of an uninterrupted sequence. But Bonnard proceeded otherwise. The attitudes of his models have none of this suspension, yet in their soft contortions they often display something of the improbable. The attitudes preferred by Bonnard are not those which suggest the past, present and future of a motion; they are complete in themselves to the extent that they appear detached from the succession of movements to which they belong. Like cats curling up at ease or stretching themselves with abandon, Bonnard's nudes seem completely relaxed, which does not mean motionless. Any connection with Degas that may appear in his work of the first decade of the twentieth century consists, as Soby has remarked, "in the adoption of awkward placing, angular motifs and abrupt cropping to create a vivid and unexpected equilibrium of forms." [40]

If Bonnard sometimes distorted or exaggerated the attitudes of his models, he did so in order to emphasize more explicitly the smoothness and balance of a movement or a gesture. He knew how to eliminate in order to insist on the particular, to dissolve outlines so that he might achieve volume through color. Thus he created, as one of his friends put it, those "rounded masses freed from the torture of the anatomists." [41] He was perfectly conscious that this arbitrary approach

Odilon Redon: *Portrait of Bonnard, 1902. Lithograph, 5¾ x
4⅞". Not included in the exhibition.*

might appear to others as faulty draftsmanship and did not even try to refute such criticisms, but he once confessed that "its faults are sometimes what gives life to a picture."[27]

Yet are they faults, these distortions? Bonnard has shown in his work that he cared little for the laws of perspective, of modeling, of anatomy, whenever they seemed to interfere with what he sought; he always felt free to attain his effects by whatever appeared most appropriate, precisely because the improbable often seemed truer to him than the probable. "When he has found the expressive gesture," wrote Lucie Cousturier, "he stretches it out, poises it, sharpens it with little touches that establish it in the light, completes it with the elements which proclaim its rhythm, underscores it, externalizes it by the artfulness of the composition, the spatting of color, the persuasive quality of the values and tones."[41] The gesture itself — probable or not — was merely a pretext for a delicate harmony of colors, and his drawing was never independent of this harmony; it was an inseparable part of the play of nuances over which Bonnard's sensuality reigned as supreme master.

Bonnard achieved this mastery the hard way: he worked from memory exclusively. Observing incessantly, he was able to store away in his memory a multitude of precise impressions and to keep his brushes richly provisioned with nothing but this wealth of recollections. The details in his paintings and the attitudes of his models are thus not merely records of what chance circumstances offered to his eyes (as they were in Vuillard's later works), they present objects or poses that struck him particularly and which he actually wanted for his compositions. Even his portraits were done in the absence of the model, as if, so to speak, the features of familiar faces were clearer before the eyes of his mind than they appeared in the presence of the person, when their mobility or incidents of light might distract him from the essential. In 1902, when Bonnard watched his brother-in-law in front of his piano, the composer's son, Charles, was sent to fetch his uncle's colors and, on a piece of paper, the painter made some color notations. Several weeks later he presented Claude Terrasse with his portrait, sober and alive, a portrait for which there had been no actual sitting at all.[42]

"Bonnard," Signac once said, "makes his own everything that nature can offer to his pictorial genius. In the little sketchbook from which he is never separated, or better still in his memory, he jots down pell-mell all that life presents to him. He understands, loves, and expresses everything he sees: the pie for dessert, the eye of his dog, a ray of sunlight coming through a window blind, the sponge in his bathtub. Then, wholly by instinct, without even attempting to give an appearance of reality to these often illegible objects, he expresses his love of life in magnificent pictures, always novel in composition, which have the unexpected flavor of unfamiliar fruits."[43]

Bonnard explained repeatedly that he did not consider himself strong enough to resist the temptations of his actual subjects and preferred to work from memory so as to concentrate better on his work. "Through attraction or primary conception," he said shortly before his death, "the painter achieves universality. It is attraction which determines the choice of motif and which conforms exactly to the picture. If this attraction, this primary conception fades away, the painter becomes dominated solely by the motif, the object before him. From that moment he ceases to create his own painting. In certain painters — Titian, for example — this conception is so strong that it never abandons them, even if they remain for a long time in direct contact with the object. But I am very weak, it is difficult for me to keep myself under control in the presence of the object."

"I often see interesting things around me," Bonnard further explained, "but for me to want to paint them they must have a particular attraction — what may be called beauty. When I paint them I try not to lose control of the primary conception; I am weak, and if I let myself go, in a moment I have lost my primary vision, I no longer know where I am going.

"The presence of the object, the motif, is very disturbing to the painter at the time he is painting. Since the starting-point of a picture is an idea, if the object is there at the moment he is working, the artist is always in danger of allowing himself to be distracted by the effects of direct and immediate vision, and to lose the primary idea on the way. Thus, after a certain period of work, the painter can no longer recover his original idea and depends on accidental qualities, he reproduces the shadows he sees . . . and such details as did not strike him at the beginning."[44]

Bonnard adopted this method of work even in his landscapes. Until about 1900 his contact with nature had been limited to his vacations in Dauphiné, mostly in the fall, and to visits in the outskirts of Paris, especially to Etang-la-Ville where Roussel settled in 1899, not far from Maurice Denis in Saint-Germain. But after the turn of the century Bonnard, who until then had fed his untiring curiosity on every aspect of Parisian life, began to divide his time equally between the country and the city. It is said that Madame Bonnard's fragile health demanded long sojourns in the country (or was it rather her shyness, her desire to flee the noisy boulevards, to escape acquaintances and even friends?) and it may also have been that the painter felt the need to develop his faculties in contact with nature, theretofore more or less neglected.

40

Left: *Claude Terrasse, 1902. Oil, 37⅜ x 30⅜". Collection Charles Terrasse, Fontainebleau.* Right: *Edouard Vuillard, 1911. Oil on wood, 18¼ x 15". Private collection, Paris. Not included in the exhibition.*

About 1903 the Bonnards began to spend their summers just outside Paris, sometimes at Montval, a stone's throw from Marly where Maillol worked, not far from either Roussel or Denis, sometimes in Vernouillet, Médan, Villennes, in all those charming little places along the meanders of the Seine between Paris and Rouen, peaceful villages hidden among trees, lazily stretched out beside the river, in which the Impressionists already had discovered numerous attractive motifs.

From the beginning Bonnard seems to have attained such an intimacy with nature that it appeared as if he had never painted anything else. But this may be explained precisely by the thoroughness with which he mentally organized his perceptions before he took up his brushes. "I liked to see," wrote his friend and admirer Lucie Cousturier, "that his enthusiasm did not lead him to pounce constantly upon his palette, but rather that he was always willing to waste time in making a choice. Moreover, the waste of time is only apparent, because he works from memory; and if he absorbs from nature, in one moment, the picture he will develop in his studio, tomorrow he will begin to ponder over the enchantment he was idly contemplating a short time before. But he never remains long in front of the motif; his essential function being to discover, he must be on the alert. . . ." [41]

Yet, in spite of his preoccupation with the primary impression, Bonnard shunned improvisations. Once, at the house of friends, he was enthusiastic about the golden richness of a tart. Asked whether he would not like to paint it, "I haven't lived long enough with this object to succeed," he replied.[54]

41

Bonnard's colors began to brighten through his new and intimate communion with nature, his brushwork gained additional freedom, a freedom that also manifests itself in other works, such as his portrait of Vuillard done in 1905, executed with rapid strokes that convey an almost sketchy character to the canvas. Yet beneath this animated surface appear a deft feeling for volumes and a superb sureness. It was the period of the *Fauves,* an echo of whom is to be found in Bonnard's broader forms, more vigorous execution and stronger colors. Nevertheless, these colors were still far from the orgies of brilliant reds, blues and yellows in which Matisse, Derain, Vlaminck then indulged. Bonnard remained primarily preoccupied with the subtle relationship of broken colors, grays and pinks, soft blues and chromes; whatever reflection the *Fauve* movement cast upon his development, was cautiously absorbed and balanced by an eye that saw nuances where the others wanted to perceive only violent clashes.

Far from desiring to impose his own will upon nature, Bonnard strove to harmonize what he called his "primary conception" with the richness of his imagination. The observation of nature was not merely a stimulating point of departure, it was the vital element upon which his self-expression throve. Thus he had fulfilled Maurice Denis' prophecy of 1895, on the occasion of a group exhibition of the Nabis: "Perhaps they will reach nature some day; that is, their conception of things may become complete enough, deep enough, that the works of art executed by them will retain all the logical harmonies which are the essential character of living nature, and that there will thus be a closer relationship between the object and the subject, between the creation and the image they will have reproduced." [45]

Many years later, Maurice Denis acknowledged that Bonnard had achieved the perfect balance — though possibly not always consciously — between what he called the two deformations: objective deformation which depends upon a purely esthetic and decorative conception, upon technical principals of coloration and composition; and subjective deformation, which brings into play the personal sensibility of the artist, his soul, his poetry, and also a certain perception of nature, which excludes, at least in theory, "literature" and abstraction. "The point is that he re-creates every scene or object with an ever-new soul," Denis explained, "obedient to his vision, an awakened sleeper, altering values, substituting for nature's logic his own logic, into which he infuses his irony or the tenderness of an awestruck observer. If one compares him with other artists who are endowed with sensitivity to color — for example, Matisse — one is amazed by all that underlies Bonnard's painting." [46]

When *Fauvism* was succeeded by Cubism, when Picasso began to emerge as the leading spirit, the most audacious, the most inventive innovator, Bonnard showed himself completely unaffected. His nature dictated another course, one which now began to draw him towards those against whom there had been a revolution in his youth, the Impressionists. If he avoided the brutality with which the *Fauves* and the Cubists deliberately altered the face of the world, his courage was no less than theirs. They often exhibited an intellectual courage while his was a visual one, unconcerned with blasting traditions but always ready to discover with innocent eyes and perpetual astonishment new aspects of forms and new relations of colors. Thus, in his own way, he extended, as they did, the limits of the impossible. He lacked neither boldness nor imagination but he endeavored to express these within the framework of a heritage which he himself broadened to the extent of his needs.

Thus preoccupied with his own efforts, Bonnard had little time to look at the work of others. When in 1906 Ranson founded an art school in which his friends promised to teach, and when, shortly afterwards, Ranson died and the friends actually took over the Académie Ranson and made it famous, Bonnard had no share in the venture. Sérusier and Denis found there a natural outlet for their pedagogical gifts, their penchant for theories. Sérusier even wrote for his pupils an *ABC de la Peinture* in which he formulated the ideas and amplified the mathematical system once elaborated by Verkade and himself (he later prided himself on having had among his pupils Roger de la Fresnaye and thus to have participated from afar in the Cubist movement). Vuillard and Roussel, on the other hand, appeared only seldom at the Académie Ranson; Vuillard modestly confessed to his pupils that he was still learning himself and Roussel preferred to read Baudelaire to them. Of Bonnard's connection with the Académie little is known; he would appear there occasionally and look at the work of the pupils, but he always avoided carefully assuming the rôle of a teacher.

Bonnard doubtless felt that there was nothing he could offer the new generation which was not contained in his own work. Painting to him was the surest way to enjoy life, and enjoyment cannot be taught. To learn the rudiments of art the beginners did not need him — any teacher would do — and beyond that only their own experience and the study of the works of others could help them to develop their own gifts. He always received young artists with paternal cordiality, but he also always declined to give advice. Hadn't he been afraid, even in his youth when they were all so excited over theories, of every influence, including his own upon others? "Nothing frightened him more than the risk of influencing someone else," said Thadée Natanson.[47] He could not even take upon himself to initiate the new generation in the secrets of draftsmanship, that standard by which so many measure the merits of a work of art. Having done away with the silhouette and proportion that convention assigns to everything, he knew that each artist must discover anew the shape of things, that it is the artist, indeed, who in the end imposes his vision upon the multitude.

The freshness and inventiveness with which Bonnard could reduce familiar features to a few exquisite lines and spots again manifested themselves about that time in his brush and ink illustrations for Jules Renard's *Histoires Naturelles*. Lautrec had already embellished Renard's short sketches with a series of remarkable lithographs, and it required no little courage on Bonnard's part to follow in the footsteps of his late friend. His drawings hold their own in comparison. No less ingenious than Lautrec but without the latter's biting irony, Bonnard created unforgettable animal personalities full of humor and tenderness. Strangely enough Jules Renard himself, who had been enchanted with Lautrec's lithographs, showed nowhere in his *Journal* the slightest appreciation of the delightful sketches with which Bonnard adorned a cheap and ordinary edition of his book. He never even mentioned them.

At the same time Bonnard also drew similarly inspired illustrations for a book by Octave Mirbeau describing a trip to Belgium, Holland and Germany in his new car, *La 628-E-8*. Though he had not accompanied the author, Bonnard did travel to Belgium, Holland, England, Italy, Spain and Tunisia between 1907 and 1911. He produced a great many charming marginal sketches for Mirbeau's book. Himself greatly interested in automobiles, Bonnard was shortly to own one which he drove, as reported by Thadée Natanson, in a rather unorthodox fashion, corresponding to the capriciousness that so often guided his behavior.

But in those years Bonnard also tackled more important projects; in fact some of the most ambitious ones he ever attempted. In 1910 he exhibited at the *Salon d'Automne* four large decorative panels for the salon of Missia Godebska, Thadée Natanson's first wife, and the following year he showed three others, executed for the Russian collector Morosoff. Once more his feeling for decorative effects combined itself with his imagination. As Bonnard later wrote to his friend George Besson: "I float between 'intimism' and decoration; one does not make oneself over." [48]

The Godebska panels, framed in fanciful, irregular borders, in which the silhouettes of gray monkeys and white and red birds stand out against a brilliant yellow ground, exhibit an idyllic life in a land of dreams. Bonnard has crowded into them an amazing number of joyful motifs: nymphs and fauns, mermaids, animals, children, lovers and even a solitary Chinese, symbols of pleasure, amusement and far-away countries. But the exuberance of his inspiration somewhat obscures the unity and drowns the various elements in a confusing richness. The sweetness as well as the simplicity of the arabesques he had achieved in earlier years is lost now that more plastic preoccupations interfere with their unfolding. Yet there is such a wealth of fantasy, of verve and even of surprise, that these panels in spite, or possibly because, of their lack of clarity, suggest a charming fairy tale told with an enchanted brush.

The three *Kakemono*-size panels which Bonnard executed the following year for Morosoff are altogether different. Under the general title "Mediterranean" they reflect the painter's first contact with the south of France. And under the impact of southern colors the arabesques are less obvious, while the decorative purpose is achieved far more successfully. Overwhelmed, as it were, by the intensity of blazing colorations that outshone those of his imagination, Bonnard now discovered in nature itself the essential elements for his composition. The harmony between what he observed and what he invented is more complete, the general effect more sober. It has been stated that one of these panels summarizes the dual nature of his painting: "Its trees and sky are rendered in the flat, silhouette style of the 1890's; but its foreground shows a naturalistic grouping of a mother and children, free of decorative artifice." [40]

Bonnard's trip to the south early in 1910 constituted a decisive factor in his development.

Illustrations for Histoires Naturelles, *1904.*

The southern landscape so deeply impressed and attracted him that from then on hardly a year passed without his spending several months on the shores of the Mediterranean. Eventually he was to settle almost permanently in the Midi, with ever shorter visits to Paris. After his first trip south, however, he merely decided to divide his life between the two landscapes he liked most: Saint-Tropez, Grasse or Le Cannet near Cannes on the one hand, and the banks of the Seine on the other. He actually purchased a small house on the Seine, in the vicinity of Vernon. This house bore the charming name of *Ma Roulotte* [My Gypsy Caravan], and the painter was careful not to change this designation which seemed so particularly suited to the vagabonding instinct of its new owner. Every day Bonnard undertook extended walks through the beautiful Seine valley and frequently also rowed his wife or his friends on the river in his small boat.

Ma Roulotte became a meeting place for Bonnard's few intimate friends who came to enjoy his company and the splendors of the landscape. Thadée Natanson, who spent many hours with him there, has drawn a lively portrait of the painter, then in his middle forties:

"This slim, active man seems tall although he stoops a little and folds up on himself, as if even his carriage means to be thoughtful. His complexion is tanned by his master the sun. He strokes his short beard which curls loosely on his obstinate chin. The faceted edges of his eyeglasses heighten the intensity of his gaze. A pair of thin lips discloses his teeth to indicate, perhaps, that his intelligent mouth is neither able nor willing to conceal anything. His fingers push his short hair back from his high forehead. He does not grow fat nor will he ever do so, in spite of his tendency to laugh; not because he refuses to rest or deliberately tries to remain thin, but because one grows stout only when vegetating on one spot, and he detests above all to let himself be tied down by anyone, to become attached or enclosed anywhere, no matter how firmly his conception of fidelity may persist; because he goes his own way with long resolute strides, following nothing but the curiosity of his wayward spirit and his imagination to which he gives free rein.

"His arms make almost random gestures which flow and die away until the pursuit of a worth-while idea redeems their aimlessness. His bearing is that of a man who likes his ease, who voluntarily adopts informal manners, but with the casualness which comes from knowing that he is ready to refortify himself at any moment. His nearsightedness is that of an observer, but it eliminates useless details. Behind his spectacles, unusually lively pupils glance over or fix upon objects in order to make them his own. His manner of listening, as well as the cautious words which express his thoughts . . . demonstrate an ability to seize upon what is characteristic and an ability to generalize, and also a capacity for paying attention and for decision, equally necessary to creators of the images which are stored up by the rest of mankind. That his hands, which are often reddened, could ever have seemed soft, is amazing when, to illustrate his words, they sketch by gestures some memory or the development of some system. . . . Nevertheless his gravity and his shyness readily melt into a smile and even welcome an opportunity to burst into laughter, which is the reason one so vividly remembers Bonnard's teeth, white and regular, as they are freely exposed. . . .

"One often finds him busy. He is also often idle. But he never seems to bustle and he never fusses. . . . Although he labors prodigiously he prefers living to working, for what is called work seems less important to him than what he calls living, that is observing and thinking in an

"Ma Roulotte" near Vernon, 1915. Oil, 22½ x 29⅛". Whereabouts unknown. Not included in the exhibition.

attempt to understand. . . . By the same token he agrees with those who prefer a man to any of his productions.

"He enjoys nothing more than to drive along the roads in an automobile, or still better to penetrate every nook and cranny of the countryside on a bicycle, or to sail on the water. . . . Sometimes, to secure a more complete change of atmosphere, he goes to some foreign country, but for a few days only, just long enough to absorb the impact and to return with highly significant photographs and characteristic souvenirs. Such excursions increase his joy in finding himself once more in Paris, among his own people and in familiar surroundings. . . .

". . . He has too much grace and too much taste for his life to exemplify to onlookers anything but the charming pattern of a philosopher untainted by proselytism, and for his numerous and delightful works, infinitely varied, in which can easily be discerned a profound knowledge of his craft as well as of the resources of his genius, ever to descend to pedantry." [47]

Bonnard's work never contravened this last prediction, published in 1912, and his knowledge of his means of expression was to develop and to improve steadily until the very end. The years before the first World War actually contributed much to the evolution of his technique. In the north Bonnard was now a neighbor of Monet, for just across the river from Vernon lies Giverny, and Bonnard frequently went there; Monet professed a great liking for him, telling visitors that he never missed any of Bonnard's exhibitions. In the south he often met Renoir, for whom he felt particular veneration and who told him on one of their walks: "Bonnard, it is necessary to embellish." By this he meant, as Bonnard later explained, "that quality which the artist should first introduce into his picture." [44] Through his friendship with both Monet and Renoir, Bonnard became aware of technical problems which seem not to have preoccupied him notably theretofore: the limpidity of Renoir's brushstroke, the nacreous quality of Monet's pigment. They were to become outstanding features of his own canvases. With the exception of Vuillard, no painter of his generation was to endow his technique with so much sensual delight, so much feeling for the undefinable texture of paint, so much vibration. The sensitivity which guided his brush he infused into every particle of paint placed on the canvas; there is almost never any dryness, any dullness in his execution. His paintings are not merely "flat surfaces covered with colors arranged in a certain order"; they are covered with colors applied with a delicate voluptuousness that confers to the pigment a life of its own and treats every single stroke like a clear note of a symphony. At the same time Bonnard's colors changed from opaque to transparent and brilliant, and his perceptiveness seemed to grow as his brush found ever more expert and more subtle means to capture the richness both of his imagination and of nature.

Bonnard's unique feeling for surface and texture also reveals itself in many of his pencil drawings in which he mingled strokes, dashes and dots in an endeavor to suggest a variety of materials or light effects. Sometimes he used erasers to create smudged planes or even rubbed the paper so vigorously that he almost perforated it; such scratched surfaces then were used to add still another quality of texture. The love and inventiveness with which Bonnard employed various mediums he also extended to etching, though here the chances for happy unorthodoxy were limited somewhat by the process of biting the plates, a process with which he was not free to interfere. Nor could he handle the exacting drypoint needle with the elegant ease to which pencils and lithographic crayons had accustomed him. When copying an original pencil sketch on copper, he was apt to lose its charm as well as its richness of tonal values. No doubt conscious of this, he practically renounced tonal values and limited himself in his engravings to purely linear expressions. Too fond of improvisations ever to explore thoroughly the intricate techniques of etching or drypoint, he was unable to exploit to their utmost the wide range of possibilities offered by copper plates. In some of his etchings, however, such as the illustrations for Mirbeau's *Dingo* and his portrait of Vollard, he demonstrated that, through a great economy of lines and subtle composition, he could achieve extremely happy results.

As if he feared to be carried away by the temptations of color, by his enchantment with atmospheric values, Bonnard began to impose upon himself the discipline of draftsmanship, just as Renoir once had done at a critical phase of his evolution. The beginning of the first World War found him sketching incessantly with pen or pencil, and about 1915 he confessed to his nephew Charles Terrasse: "I have sent myself back to school. I want to forget all I know; I am trying to learn what I do not know. I am restarting my studies from the beginning, from ABC ... and I am on guard against myself, against everything that used to thrill me so much, against the color that bewilders you. . . ."

Left: *Illustration for* Dingo, *1923. Etching, 11¼ x 8⅞".*
Right: *Ambroise Vollard, c. 1914* (?). *Etching, 14 x 9⁷⁄₁₆". Private collection, New York.*

And a little later he stated: "I think I have found it. Certainly I had been carried away by color. I was almost unconsciously sacrificing form to it. But it is true that form exists and that one cannot arbitrarily and indefinitely reduce or transpose it; it's drawing, then, that I need to study. . . . I draw constantly. And after drawing comes composition, which should form a balance. A well-composed picture is half completed. And such is the art of composition that with nothing but black and white, a pencil, a pen, an engraver's burin, one can achieve results that are almost as complete and fine in quality as can be produced by a whole palette of colors. . . ." [49]

Bonnard emerged from this examination of his own conscience with stronger linear accents in his compositions, with subjects that favored sharp angles or repetitions of horizontals and verticals, with a greater emphasis upon stability. His work executed between approximately 1915 and 1920 often indicates these preoccupations, but once the new problems were mastered he permitted himself to respond again to the seduction of color. And he actually achieved a greater intensity of color than ever before. His paintings of the 1920's, while not returning immediately to the soft, blurred outlines that had distinguished many of his works done in the first decade of the twentieth century, appear less insistent on linear structure mainly because their rich, glowing colors again form the center of attention. But behind their intense and opalescent coloration

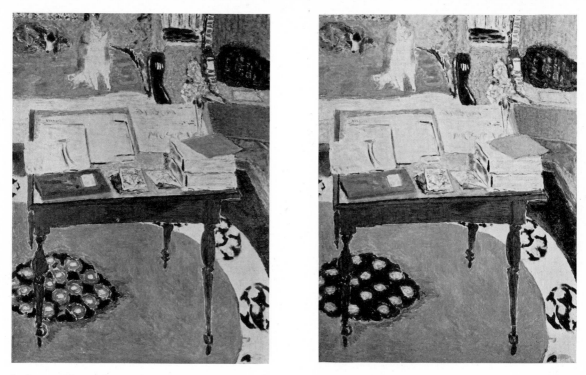

Left: *Table with Music Album, photographed 1926 before being retouched.*
Right: *Table with Music Album, 1926-32. Oil, 48 x 36". Private collection, New York.*

lies a new feeling for plasticity, a new strength that appears in such masterpieces as "La chevelure d'or" of 1924 (*page 101*), and "The Palm" of 1926 (*page 102*).

In the course of this process one feature almost completely disappeared from Bonnard's work: the underlying irony that so often added a particular charm to his paintings. His new maturity aimed higher and did away with the narrative tendencies of his brush. Instead, a much rarer quality is found in his work, a quality achieved only by the great: serenity. Above the accidental and the unexpected, it embodies the deep wisdom of a soul at peace with itself and the world.

Serenity does not mean self-satisfaction. Bonnard always was highly critical of his own output. He liked to exchange views with Vuillard upon the merits of their respective works, but each of the two painters remained his own most severe judge. Seldom completely satisfied, Bonnard liked to retouch his canvases again and again, often many years after their completion (as for instance his "Table with Music Album" where, as an afterthought, he simplified the design of the rug. It has been reported that during his visits to the Luxembourg Museum in Paris, where one of his own paintings hung, he would take out a small paint-box and add a few touches to the picture, unobserved by the guards, whose attention was being distracted by Vuillard. Bonnard once said that he worked "brush in one hand, rag in the other." But in his self-criticism he proceeded without any pomposity, modestly declaring that one should judge a painting "as a milliner judges the hat she is making." [27] The pleasure of the eye seemed again to be the sole criterion for his approval.

"A painting," Bonnard said towards the end of his life, "is a series of spots which are joined together and ultimately form the object, the unit over which the eye wanders without obstruction." [50] There is no longer any mention of draftsmanship in this definition, no mention even of the "certain order" which Denis had advocated for the arrangement of colors on a flat surface.

How Bonnard proceeded in assembling this series of spots was witnessed once by Félix Fénéon who, after the *Revue Blanche* discontinued publication in 1903, had joined the Bernheim-Jeunes, where he actively assisted Bonnard's ever-growing reputation. Accompanying the painter on one of his trips south (in 1925 Bonnard bought a small house in Le Cannet), Fénéon later told how he had watched him at work:

"With four thumb-tacks he had pinned a canvas, lightly tinted with ocher, to the dining-room wall. During the first few days he would glance from time to time, as he painted, at a sketch on a piece of paper twice the size of one's hand, on which he had made notes in oil, pencil, and ink of the dominant colors of each little section of the motif. At first I could not identify the subject. Did I have before me a landscape or a seascape? On the eighth day (until then I had no doubt failed to inspect the canvas), I was astonished to be able to recognize a landscape in which a house appeared in the distance and a young woman on a path, with a child and two dogs beside her. From that time on Bonnard no longer referred to his sketch. He would step back to judge the effect of the juxtaposed tones; occasionally he would place a dab of color with his finger, then another next to the first. On about the fifteenth day I asked him how long he thought it would take him to finish his landscape. Bonnard replied: 'I finished it this morning.' " [51]

Instead of working at an easel, it was Bonnard's habit to tack pieces of canvas directly on the wall. Sometimes these pieces were rather big, and he would execute simultaneously on this broad surface several paintings of totally different subjects. The astonished visitor thus would perceive at the same time a large study of a woman stretched out in a bathtub and, separated by the narrowest white strip, a standing nude, while elsewhere on the same piece of canvas Bonnard had embarked on a small still life. Once finished, they would be cut apart and mounted on stretchers.

Usually Bonnard made a preliminary charcoal sketch on his canvas and then set out first to establish the green values. Little by little he raised the tonalities, not hesitating to use black, which he well knew how to apply in such a manner that it would miraculously pull the bright tones together. Having observed that scenes often look like mosaics spotted with light and dark — that is to say with bright colors and violet shadows — he showed an increasing tendency to handle form and color tapestry-fashion, the near and the far distance inseparably interwoven into a flat surface of vibrating tones.

Bonnard seemed completely indifferent to the surroundings in which he worked. Many a time his work was done in drab hotel rooms, and even in his own house at Le Cannet he did not possess a studio; he painted in a small room which scarcely afforded the space he needed to step back and judge the work done, and which was astonishingly devoid of painters' gear. On the table a nicked plate covered with more or less dirty colors represented the source of the artist's luminous tones. Comfort and environment counted little for this man whose entire creative effort

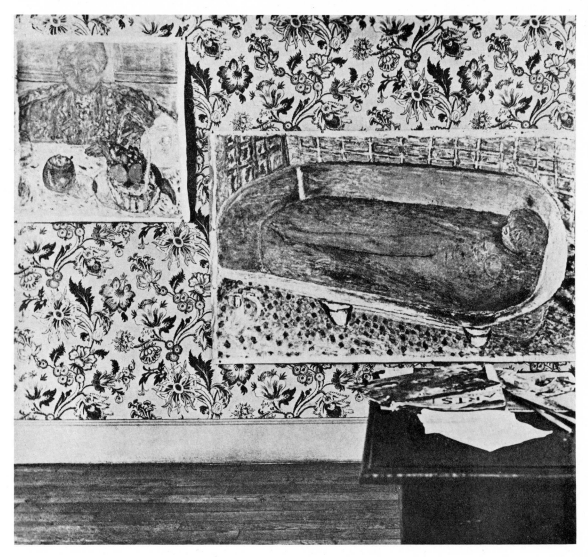

Wall of Bonnard's Room in Deauville, 1937. Photograph Rogi André, Verve.

was accomplished in front of indifferent or even hostile walls. Face to face with them, turning his side or his back to the source of light and to the room in which he worked, distracted by nothing around him, thinking solely of his "primary conception," Bonnard seemed to isolate himself from his surroundings so as better to concentrate upon his work. And in this silent struggle with the wall that faced him, that actually barred the horizon, that seemed to provoke him, the flight of his imagination became Bonnard's unique weapon with which to master the unholy emptiness of the canvas which he had fixed upon it.

When painting in hotel rooms, Bonnard frequently tacked his pieces of canvas against walls papered with loud and flowery designs that brutally clashed with his delicate harmonies. It was not that he was unaware of their vociferous presence, but he quietly accepted their challenge, somewhat mindful of the fact that his finished paintings might some day have to contend with similar surroundings on a collector's wall. And the purity of his colors always gained the upper hand, for their beguiling freshness could not be harmed by the vulgarity of any wallpapers.

The freshness and the lyricism of Bonnard's work are qualities which are not always apparent to the observer at first sight. His paintings were never destined for museums; he used to say that "the museums are filled with homeless works." [27] The place for his canvases is a living-room where friendly eyes can return to them again and again until every luminous patch of color has begun to sing in its proper key. Doubtless it was this necessity for prolonged, even loving observation, together with the absence of all sensational effects, which prevented Bonnard's work for many years from reaching the crowds, the large public beyond the circle of enlightened collectors. It seems significant, however, that those who lived with his paintings were seldom satisfied with one and gradually built up large collections of his pictures. Among these the Hahnloser Collection in Winterthur, Switzerland, and that of Mr. and Mrs. Duncan Phillips in Washington, D. C., deserve special mention.

Though Bonnard's paintings were included in exhibitions all over the world, many years passed before he was accorded the status of a master. At Pittsburgh in 1923 he had to be content with a third prize at the 22nd Carnegie International Exhibition. Three years later he was invited to be a member of a Carnegie jury where he waged a vigorous battle on behalf of Roussel, for whom he obtained a second prize. During his brief stay in this country Bonnard went to see some public and private collections, including those of Mr. and Mrs. Ralph M. Coe in Cleveland and the Phillips Memorial Gallery in Washington (he immediately asked Mr. Duncan Phillips for a brush and colors in order to retouch one of his own paintings). From his short visit to the United States, Bonnard brought away with him an impression of furious speed and overwhelming hospitality.

In 1936 Bonnard was awarded a second Carnegie prize while the first went to Leon Kroll. Bonnard was too modest to decline this humiliating "honor," but he always refused to solicit any distinctions and for this reason — like Vuillard, Roussel and Vallotton — was never decorated with the red ribbon of the Legion of Honor.

Paying no attention whatsoever to his "career," he lived a quiet, uneventful life in which the only conspicuous milestones were his works. The pattern of the passing years varied little in their alternation between north and south, but Bonnard's sojourns in Paris itself tended to grow shorter. From 1930 to 1932 he went to Arcachon, while in the following years he preferred Deauville and Trouville. At the outbreak of the second World War he retired to his house at Le Cannet and did not return to Paris until after its liberation, in 1945. During the years of occupation, when oil and paints were almost unobtainable, he worked frequently with watercolors and gouache and achieved great mastery in these mediums, which he had begun to use about 1925 but, until the war, had resorted to only on rare occasions. As to his subjects, they remained the same: landscapes, still lifes, nudes, an occasional portrait or self portrait. He also worked on some decorative compositions and painted a "Saint François" commissioned for a village church in Haute-Savoie. But in general human beings became ever fewer in his paintings.

Bonnard's pink house at Le Cannet, shrouded by greenery, dominates a hill down which orange, olive, and almond trees cascade in terraces to the Mediterranean. The painter was par-

Still Life of Fruit, c. 1925-30. Pencil, 11¾ x 13¼". Private collection, Zurich.

ticularly fond of mimosas. He would not tolerate the hand of man in nature, and as a result his garden was overgrown, its narrow paths almost choked with wild plants and flowers. Behind the house are more gardens and terraces watered by a canal whose banks furnished a walk for Bonnard's favorite promenade, a promenade on which he was always accompanied by his basset. There, looking at the hills, Bonnard recalled the Ile-de-France countryside laced by the wide ribbon of the Seine.

People who visited him in his pink house found an unpretentious man who offered a kindly welcome while he observed them, through his thick glasses, with a glint of humor. He liked to show them two small works by Renoir dedicated to him and to comment admiringly upon the unequaled mastery of his friend. When asked for advice, now, in the evening of his life, he was sometimes more explicit than he had been before. In 1945 he even wrote a few words of introduction for an exhibition of Gaston Agasse, held at the little gallery of his old friend, Jacques Rodrigues-Henriques.

"You are right," he wrote to a young painter, "to concern yourself with drawing, which consists of the definition of forms. . . . Go in for large dimensions, they will show up your merits and your faults more clearly." And he added: "As for colors, use only a very few pigments for each work; look at chromos, labels, posters." [52] Thus, towards the end of his life, he must have felt that his own beginnings, with lithographs and posters, had started him in the right direction.

The Model, c. 1938. Pencil, 20½ x 14⅝". Private collection, France.

He went even further and told some visitors: "I'm an old man now and I begin to see that I do not know any more than I knew when I was young." This statement, notwithstanding its modesty, was to some extent true.

Since the outset, despite the evolution of his art, Bonnard had remained the same. And in spite of all the knowledge accumulated over more than fifty years, his art still sprang less from things he had learned than from the ones he carried within himself, from his ability to absorb the spectacle of nature and to re-create it according to the logic of his imagination. He continued to observe incessantly, and for him to observe still meant to enjoy. But there was more than mere enjoyment behind his art, more than just subtlety, good nature and sometimes humor. He achieved the power of those who devote all their abilities to a unique goal, and the serenity that eventually crowns single-minded effort. The works of his last years are not inferior to his early ones in freshness and spontaneity, but their horizon is broadened and their color more intense than ever before. Bonnard gradually extended the gamut of his colorations while at the same time he carried his forms closer to abstraction.

Interior, c. 1938. Pencil, 9⅞ x 12⅝". Private collection, France.

    In his modesty, Bonnard even found a typical explanation for the more complete realisation of his later work. "When one is young," he said, "one becomes enthralled with a place, a motif, an object discovered by accident; it is this enthusiasm that makes one paint. Later one works differently, guided by the need to express a sentiment; one chooses then a point of departure more closely connected with one's own abilities." [55]

    The brush which formerly seemed to have caressed the canvas became febrile and fervid in the hand of the old master. It accumulated colors vividly on the canvas, as if there were no time left for the mellowness of pigment that had once been its characteristic. Bonnard now favored thin paint as had done the aging Renoir and often disregarded structure as did Monet during his last decades. Forms seemed to disappear behind a dense tissue of color spots, compositions were simplified, lines became looser. The successor and last survivor of Impressionism, Bonnard carried on a glorious tradition, revitalized through the harmonious interplay of acute observation, happy imagination and innate lyricism. His ultimate message was the apotheosis of color, as if he felt that in these troubled times it would bring salvation. Thus he "purified" his art until it was nothing but the vibrant expression of feasts of harmonies gradually raised in volume, harmonies derived from nature but transposed and amplified to the point where the motif seemed to disappear for the sake of sheer color. He liked to speak of light, "that southern light during certain hours, which — over great spaces — becomes the principal subject of a sensitive artist."[53] "Our God is light," he told a young painter. "A day will come when you will understand what that means."

In 1940, while their country lay helplessly defeated, Bonnard's wife had died and left him alone, grieving, bewildered and almost lost in a world whose energies seemed devoted solely to destruction. A great emptiness made itself felt around the old man who, with the friendship of only a few, had built his small and peaceful universe. The German occupation scattered his friends; some, like Natanson, the Bernheim-Jeunes and Besson went into hiding; others perished, unable to endure the tragedy of the war, like Vuillard who died after a disastrous flight, surviving Pétain's armistice by only a few days. Fewer and fewer became those around whom Bonnard's sequestered life had gravitated. Vollard had succumbed; Roussel, Fénéon, Maurice Denis, and Maillol soon followed. Bonnard lived to witness the defeat of Germany, but he also witnessed these constant losses that painfully accentuated his loneliness.

He went on painting at Le Cannet. Was there anything else he could have done? His last work was a small canvas of a flowering almond tree (*page 134*). He had barely signed it when he closed his eyes on January 23, 1947. The newly born Fourth Republic which had just accorded national funerals to a great poet and a musician seemed almost unaware that it had lost one of its greatest painters. But then the pomp of an official burial would not have been consistent with Bonnard's life. No painter actually has ever been honored on his deathbed by the nation that for the last two hundred years has given the world its greatest artists. No painter has ever been admitted to its national shrine of the Panthéon. Thus, as it were, tradition demanded that only a few relatives, friends and neighbors should accompany Bonnard to his last rest, that no member of the Cabinet should be present, no museum official speak a few words of farewell. But nature bemoaned the passing away of the master who so incessantly had glorified its splendors. And as a sign of mourning, on the day of his burial, it covered these splendors, the yellow brilliance of the mimosas, the pinkish brightness of the almond trees that he had loved so much, with a delicate veil of fresh snow.

57

Notes to the Text

1. Bonnard, undated letter to his grandmother; Bonnard: Correspondances, Paris, 1944, p. 11.

2. Dom W. Verkade: Le Tourment de Dieu, Paris, 1926, p. 75-76. Quotations from this book were translated from the French version, supervised by the author, instead of being taken from the not always adequately translated English edition: Yesterdays of an Artist Monk, London, 1930.

3. Gauguin, letter to Denis [June 1899]; Lettres de Gauguin à sa femme et à ses amis, Paris, 1946, p. 290-91.

4. Verkade, op. cit., p. 70.

5. Verkade, ibid., p. 80.

6. A. Fontainas: Bonnard, introduction to Album d'Art Druet, Paris.

7. Sérusier, letter to Denis, 1889; Sérusier: ABC de la Peinture, suivie d'une étude sur la vie et l'oeuvre de Paul Sérusier, par Maurice Denis, Paris, 1942, p. 47.

8. See Natanson quoted by C. Roger-Marx: Vuillard et son temps, Paris, 1945, p. 14, and M. Denis: L'époque du Symbolisme, Gazette des Beaux-Arts, March 1934.

9. M. Denis: Théories, 1890-1910, Paris, 1912, p. 9 [article published in 1890].

10. Ibid., p. 27 [article published in 1895].

11. Ibid., p. 1 [article published in 1890].

12. Ibid., p. 163 [article published in 1903].

13. From an unpublished manuscript by T. Natanson: Le Bonnard que je vous offre.

14. Bonnard, letter to Lugné-Poë [1890]; Lugné-Poë: La Parade I, Le Sot du Tremplin, Paris, 1930, p. 242-43.

15. Ibid., p. 195.

16. Ibid., p. 213-14 [article published 1891 in Art et Critique].

17. A. Aurier: Le symbolisme en peinture — Paul Gauguin, Mercure de France, March 1891.

18. Camille Pissarro commented on Aurier's article in a letter to his son Lucien: "You will observe how tenuous is the logic of this littérateur. According to him what in the last instance can be dispensed with in a work of art is drawing or painting; only ideas are essential, and these can be indicated by a few symbols. — Now I will grant that art is as he says, except that "the few symbols" have to be drawn, after all; moreover it is also necessary to express ideas in terms of color, hence you have to have sensations in order to have ideas. . . ." Pissarro: Letters to his Son Lucien, New York, 1943, p. 163-64.

19. A. Aurier: Les Symbolistes, Revue Encyclopédique, April 1, 1892.

20. R. Marx: Exhibition review in Le Voltaire, October 1, 1892.

21. M. Denis: op. cit., p. 21 [article published in 1895].

22. M. Denis [pseud. Pierre Louis]: Pour les jeunes peintres, Art et Critique, February 20, 1892. In 1898 Bonnard was to reply to a questionnaire: "I think that competitions have never, or almost never, produced anything worth while. A jury in general has nothing to do with a work commissioned for his own use by an industrialist or dealer. The client himself should look for an artist who can satisfy him; he will have no trouble finding one in Paris." (L'Estampe et l'Affiche, 1898, p. 87.)

23. Lugné-Poë: La Parade II, Acrobaties, Souvenirs et Impressions de Théâtre, 1894-1902, Paris, 1932, p. 50.

24. Quoted by R. Goldwater: Symbolist Art and Theater: Vuillard, Bonnard, Maurice Denis, Magazine of Art, Dec. 1946.

25. R. Marx: Les Indépendants, Le Voltaire, March 28, 1893.

26. See A. Vollard: Souvenirs d'un marchand de tableaux, Paris, 1937, p. 299.

27. Carnet de Bonnard in Verve, vol. V, Nos. 17-18, 1947.

28. A. Mellerio: La lithographie en couleurs, Paris, 1898, p. 9.

29. G. Geffroy: Pierre Bonnard, Le Journal, Jan. 8, 1896.

30. Camille Pissarro: Letters to his Son Lucien, New York, 1943, p. 281-82. [Letter dated Feb. 6, 1896.]

31. Mellerio, op. cit., p. 23-24.

32. Ibid., p. 9.

33. In 1894 F. Hérold had presented Paphnutius with sets by Ranson, Roussel and Vuillard to a small audience which comprised Mallarmé, Valéry, Debussy and Pierre Louys. At about the same time Maillol painted sets for the Théâtre des Marionettes of Maurice Bouchor, a friend of Verlaine and Puvis de Chavannes (see J. Cladel: Maillol, Paris, 1937, p. 41-42).

34. Bonnard liked to model occasionally and had a large ornamental table centerpiece cast in bronze; it was exhibited in 1902 at Vollard's. He also did some cabinet-making and pyrographic work, notably for the wooden frame of one of his screens.

35. See Sérusier's letter to Verkade in Denis' biographical study, op. cit., p. 75.

36. G. Geffroy: Premier Salon, *Le Journal*, March 15, 1899.

37. Thiébault-Sisson: Un Salon d'avant-garde, *Le Temps*, March 24, 1899.

38. See P. Signac: Fragments du Journal [Feb. 9, 1909], *Arts de France*, Nos. 17-18, 1947.

39. A. Gide: Promenade au Salon d'Automne, *Gazette des Beaux-Arts*, Dec. 1905.

40. From an unpublished manuscript by James T. Soby: Bonnard and Vuillard.

41. L. Cousturier: Bonnard, *L'Art Décoratif*, Dec. 20, 1912.

42. See C. Terrasse: Bonnard, Paris, 1927, p. 73-74.

43. P. Signac: Les besoins individuels et la peinture *in* Encyclopédie Française, vol. XVI, ch. II, Paris, 1935.

44. A. Lamotte: Le bouquet de roses; propos de Pierre Bonnard, recueillis en 1943, *Verve*, vol. V, Nos. 17-18, 1947.

45. Denis: Théories, p. 29-30 [article published in 1895].

46. Denis: L'époque du Symbolisme, *Gazette des Beaux-Arts*, March 1934.

47. T. Natanson: Pierre Bonnard, *La Vie*, June 15, 1912.

48. Bonnard, letter to G. Besson, c. 1944, quoted by S. Fumet: Bonnard comme expression française de la peinture, *Formes et Couleurs*, No. 2, 1944.

49. Terrasse, *op. cit.*, p. 127-130.

50. Tériade: Propos de Pierre Bonnard, *Verve*, vol. V, Nos. 17-18, 1947.

51. Fénéon quoted by A. Charpentier, introduction to the catalog of an exhibition: Bonnard, Laprade, Bouche, Durand-Ruel Galleries, Paris, 1939.

52. Bonnard, letter to Mlle D. M., 1941, quoted in *Le Point*, No. XXIV, 1943 [special issue: Bonnard] p. 44.

53. Bonnard, introduction to the exhibition of works by Gaston Stephane Agasse, Galerie Jacques Rodrigues-Henriques, Paris, Dec. 1945.

54. H. Hahnloser-Bühler: Felix Vallotton et ses amis, Paris, 1936, p. 265.

55. *Ibid.*, p. 93-94.

Study of a Red Partridge, 1889. Oil, 8¾ x 6¼″. Collection Raoul de Ricci, Paris.

60

The Parade, 1890. Oil, 9 x 12⅝″. Private collection, Switzerland. Not included in the exhibition.

Intimacy, c. 1891. Oil, 15 x 14¼". Collection Charles Terrasse, Fontainebleau.

*The Checkered Blouse, 1892. Oil, 24 x 13". Collection
Charles Terrasse, Fontainebleau.*

Screen, c. 1891-92. Four panels, tempera on cloth mounted on wood, 63 x 20″ each. Collection Louis Carré.

Screen, c. 1892-95. Four panels, 56¼ x 17¾" each. Private collection, France. Not included in the exhibition.

Street in Eragny (Oise), c. 1894. Oil on wood, 13⅜ x 10¼". Collection Captain Edward Molyneux, Paris.

Roofs, c. 1895-1900. Oil, 13⅞ x 15⅛″. Collection Dr. and Mrs. David M. Levy, New York.

The Cab Horse, Boulevard des Batignolles, c. 1895. Oil on wood, 11¾ x 15¾". Collection Captain Edward Molyneux, Paris.

At the Moulin Rouge, 1896. Oil, 23½ x 16". Collection Wright Ludington, Santa Barbara, California.

Nude with Raised Arm, 1898. Oil on wood, 16⅛ x 23¼". Collection Henry Decoin, Paris.

70

Luncheon Table, c. 1900. Oil, 19½ x 25¾". Cone Collection, bequest of Frederic W. Cone to The Baltimore Museum of Art.

Street Scene, 1900. Oil, 13 x 23". French Art Galleries, Inc., New York.

Movement in the Street, 1900. Oil, 14 x 19". Phillips Memorial Gallery, Washington, D. C.

Portrait of a Woman, c. 1906. Oil on wood, 20 x 16". Collection Mr. and Mrs. Leo Glass, New York.

The Lunch, 1906. Oil, 24 x 36¼". Private collection, Paris.

74

The Loge (Gaston and Josse Bernheim-Jeune and their wives), 1908. Oil, 35½ x 47¼". Private collection Bernheim-Jeune, Paris.

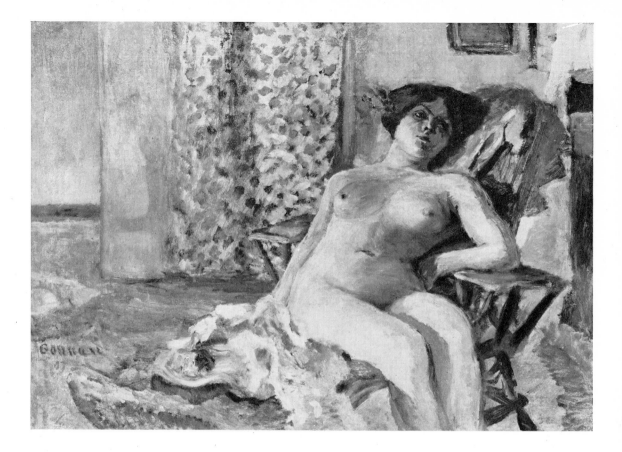

Model in an Armchair, c. 1907. Oil on wood, 24 x 32¼". Collection Jacques Lindon, New York.

La Bouillabaisse, *c. 1910. Oil, 24¾ x 12¼". Collection Mrs. Hedy Hahnloser-Bühler, Winterthur.*

The Pont de Grenelle and the Eiffel Tower, c. 1912 (?) . Oil, 21¼ x 26¾". Private collection, Paris.

Opposite: *The Boulevard, c. 1904. Oil, 32 x 16½". Jacques Seligmann and Co., New York.*

In a Southern Garden, 1913. Oil, 33 x 44½". Kunstmuseum, Berne.

Opposite page: Siesta — The Artist's Studio, c. 1910. Oil, 43 x 51½". Collection Mrs. S. Kaye, England.

Tugboat on the Seine near Rolleboise, c. 1912 (?). Oil, 22 x 31". Collection Mrs. John Work Garrett, Baltimore.

*Boating on the Seine (Madame Bonnard), 1915. Oil, 22 x 20". Collection Sam
Salz, New York.*

Woman Washing Herself, 1916. Oil, 16 x 16⅞". Private collection Bernheim-Jeune, Paris.

Opposite: *The Source — Kneeling Bather, c. 1917. Oil, 32 x 17¼". Private collection, Paris.*

L'Estérel, c. 1917. Oil, 22 x 28¾". Stedelijk Museum, Amsterdam.

Abduction of Europa, 1919. Oil, 46¼ x 60¼". The Toledo Museum of Art, Toledo, Ohio.

Nude in Front of a Fireplace, 1919. Oil, 46½ x 19¼". Kunstverein, Winterthur.

Dressing Table and Mirror, c. 1920. Oil, 49¼ x 43⅜". Private collection, Lugano.

Still Life with Basket of Bananas, 1923. Oil, 24 x 25½". Private collection,Switzerland.

Still Life with Petroleum Lamp, 1921. Oil, 28⅜ x 34¼". Private collection, Zurich.

The Open Window, 1921. Oil, 46½ x 34¾". Phillips Memorial Gallery, Washington, D. C.

The Riviera — Large Midi Landscape, 1923. Oil, 31 x 30". Phillips Memorial Gallery, Washington, D. C.

Signac and His Friends Sailing, 1924. Oil, 48⅞ x 54¾". Kunsthaus, Zurich. Not included in the exhibition.

Village Scene, c. 1925-30. Oil, 28¾ x 20½". Private collection through the courtesy of the Worcester Art Museum, Worcester, Massachusetts.

Portrait of Madame Bonnard, c. 1925. Oil, 30½ x 19¾". Private collection, France.

Woman and Dog, 1922. Oil, 27 x 15½". Phillips Memorial Gallery, Washington, D. C.

The Dining Room, 1925. Oil, 50½ x 74″. Private collection.

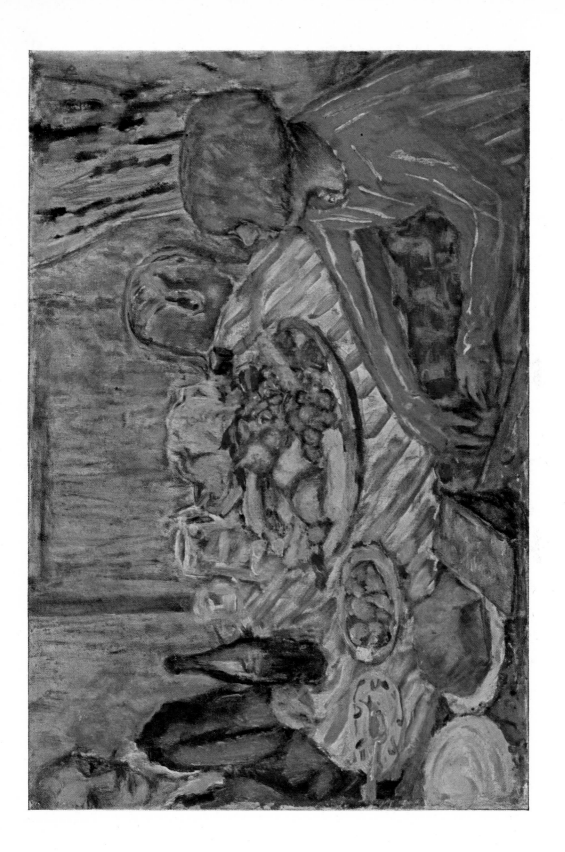

Luncheon, c. 1927. Oil, 16¼ x 24½". The Museum of Modern Art, New York. Given anonymously.

La chevelure d'or, *c. 1924. Oil, 26½ x 21". Private collection, New York.*

The Palm, 1926. Oil, 44 x 57½". Phillips Memorial Gallery, Washington, D. C.

Table with Music Album, 1926-32. Oil, 48 x 36". Private collection, New York.

The Road to Nantes, c. 1930. Oil, 26¾ x 25⅝". Collection Leonard C. Hanna, Jr., Cleveland.

104

Strawberries, 1928. Oil, 10½ x 10″. Collection Mrs. Duncan Phillips, Washington, D. C.

Le pot provençal, *1930. Oil, 29¾ x 24½". Collection Mrs. Hedy Hahnloser-Bühler, Winterthur.*

Bowl with Fruit, 1930. Oil, 18½ x 12¼". Private collection, Paris.

Left: *Still Life, 1930-31. Gouache, 6½ x 5⅛". Private collection, France.*

Right: *The French Window (Arcachon), 1930-31. Gouache, 6¼ x 5⅛". Private collection, France.*

108

Breakfast Room (Arcachon), 1930-31. Oil, 63¼ x 44⅛". The Museum of Modern Art, New York. Given anonymously.

Interior with View of Landscape, c. 1930-35. Oil, 42⅜ x 25". Collection Mr. and Mrs. Sam A. Lewisohn, New York.

110

The Checkered Dress, 1928. Oil, 30⅞ x 18⅝". Collection Mr. and Mrs. Laurence S. Rockefeller, New York.

Landscape of the Midi, c. 1930. Oil, 24⅝ x 32". Smith College Museum of Art, Northampton, Massachusetts.

112

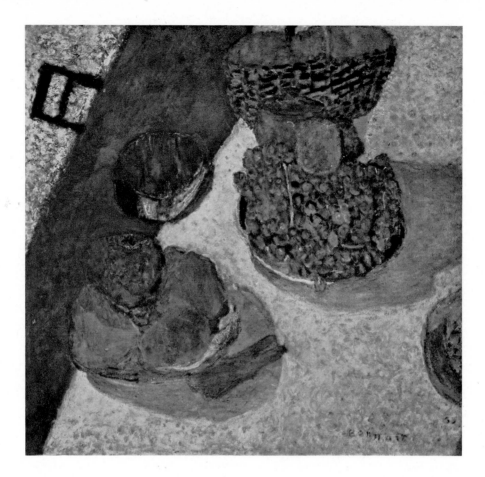

Corner of a Table, c. 1935. Oil, 65¾ x 64⅜″. Musée d'Art Moderne, Paris.

White Interior, 1933. Oil, 43 x 63¾". Musée de Grenoble.

114

Breakfast, 1932. Oil, 26¾ x 32⅝". Musée d'Art Moderne de la Ville de Paris, Petit Palais, Paris. Not included in the exhibition.

Dinner Table and Garden, 1934. Oil, 49 x 52½". Solomon R. Guggenheim Foundation, New York. Not included in the exhibition.

116

Cabinet de toilette, *1932. Oil, 47¼ x 47¼". Collection Mr. and Mrs. Samuel A. Marx, Chicago.*

Dish with Fruit, 1933. Oil, 22¾ x 20¾". Collection Mrs. William M. Elkins, Philadelphia.

Still Life with Fruit, 1936. Oil, 14¼ x 24". Collection Mr. and Mrs. Joseph Pulitzer, Jr., St. Louis.

Landscape, 1933. Oil, 42⅛ x 24¾". Kunstverein, Winterthur.

120

Self Portrait, 1938. Oil, 23 x 26⅜″. Collection Georges Wildenstein, New York.

The Mediterranean at Saint-Tropez, 1936. Oil, 18 x 22". Collection Sam Salz, New York.

Mediterranean, c. 1935 (?) . Gouache, 9¾ x 13". Smith College Museum of Art, Northampton, Massachusetts.

Still Life, Preparation for Lunch, 1940. Gouache, 20¼ x 26". The Art Institute of Chicago.

Below: Interior — Dining Room, 1942-46. Oil, 32¾ x 39⅜". Private collection, France. Not in exhibition.

124

The Checkered Tablecloth, 1936. Oil, 28½ x 30″. Private collection, New York.

Nude in a Bathtub, 1938-43. Oil, 48⅜ x 59⅞". Private collection, Paris.

128

Dark Nude, 1943-45. Oil, 31⅞ x 25⅝". Collection Louis Carré, Paris.

The Harbor of Trouville, 1938-46. Oil, 30¼ x 40½". Musée d'Art Moderne, Paris.

Below: Circus Horse, 1946. Oil, 37 x 46½". Collection Charles Terrasse, Fontainebleau.

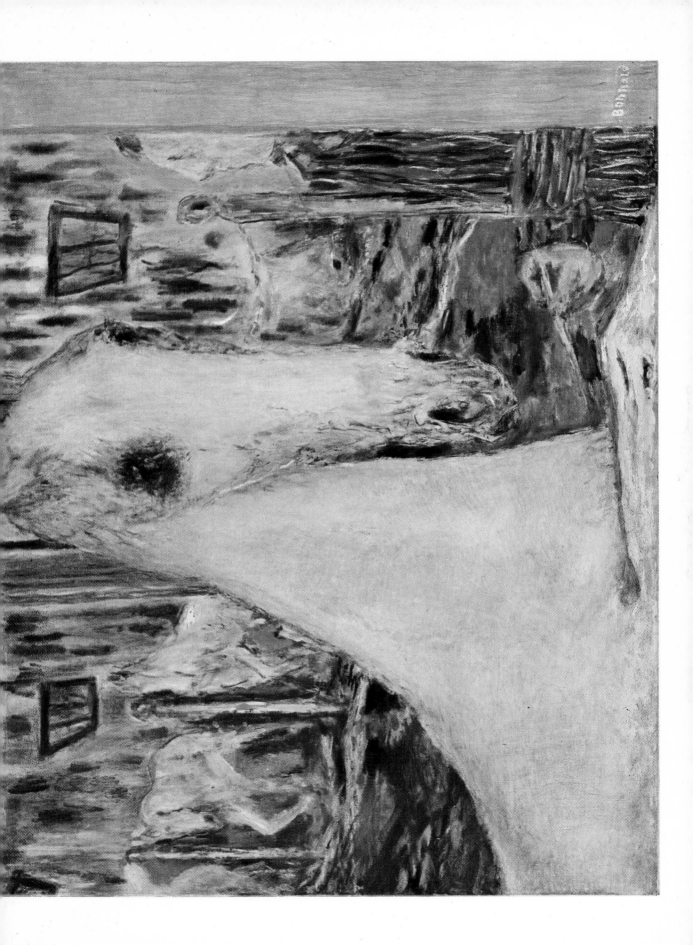

Stiff Ascent at Le Cannet, 1945. Oil, 23⅝ x 28¾". Collection Louis Carré, Paris.

Flowering Almond-Tree, 1946-47. Oil, 17¼ x 15". Private collection, France.

1867 Oct. 13, Pierre Bonnard is born at Fontenaye-aux-Roses, second child of Eugène Bonnard and Elise Mertzdorff.

c.1877 is put into a boarding school; later goes to Lycées de Vanves and Louis-le-Grand.

c.1885 after his baccalaureate studies law at the insistence of his father.

1888 works at the Ecole des Beaux-Arts, competes unsuccessfully for the Prix de Rome. Interested in Japanese prints. Studies at the Académie Jullian, Faubourg St. Denis, where he meets Denis, Vuillard, Ranson, Sérusier. In October Sérusier returns from Brittany and reveals Gauguin's art to his friends. The "Nabis" begin to gather regularly. Bonnard fails in oral law examinations, works in Government office.

1889 lives 8 rue de Parme in Paris with his grandmother. Sells champagne poster for 100 francs and decides to become an artist. First studio rue Lechapelais in Batignolles quarter. Gauguin's exhibition at the Café Volpini is decisive factor in his evolution. 1889-90, military service.

1890 studio: 28 rue Pigalle with Vuillard and Denis later joined by Lugné-Poë. Bonnard's work is noticed by Lautrec. His sister marries Claude Terrasse.

1891 shows 5 canvases and 4 decorative panels at the *Indépendants* and exhibits in the fall with his friends in Saint-Germain as well as at Le Barc de Boutteville's. Is noticed by Geffroy. The *Revue Blanche* is founded by the Natanson brothers. Drawings by Bonnard and the other Nabis appear in 1891-92 in *La Vie Moderne*. Gauguin leaves for Tahiti.

1892 shows 7 canvases at the *Indépendants*, also exhibits with his friends in Saint-Germain and at Le Barc de Boutteville's. His work is noticed by Roger Marx and Aurier. Designs sets for the Théâtre d'Art.

1893 studio: 65 rue de Douai. Exhibits at the *Indé-pendants* and in group show at Le Barc de Boutteville's. Contributes lithographs to the *Revue Blanche* and *L'Escarmouche*. Roussel marries Vuillard's sister. 1893-94, Lugné-Poë founds his Théâtre de l'Oeuvre. Vollard opens a small gallery rue Laffitte; Bonnard meets Vollard through Denis.

1894 Thadée Natanson buys paintings by Bonnard who exhibits at the *Indépendants* and in group show at Le Barc de Boutteville's.

1895 Vollard publishes "Quelques aspects de la vie de Paris" and exhibits these lithographs together with works by Lautrec and Vallotton. Tiffany shows at the Salon a series of stained glass windows, among them one after a design by Bonnard.

1896 first one-man show at Durand-Ruel's (49 paintings, some posters, lithographs, etc.). Claude Terrasse settles in Paris. With Terrasse works for "Théâtre des Pantins" and for the presentation of *Ubu-Roi* at the Théâtre de l'Oeuvre. Is invited with Lautrec and Vuillard to show with *La Libre Esthétique* in Brussels but does not send work in time.

1897 participates in group show at Vollard's; shows lithographs at *La Libre Esthétique*. Illustrates Peter Nansen's *Marie* for the *Revue Blanche*. Sérusier elaborates new theories in which Bonnard shows no interest.

1898 participates in group show at Vollard's; represented in exhibition of French Art (van Gogh, Gauguin, Bonnard, Vuillard) in Oslo, Stockholm, Göteborg. Models marionettes for Franc-Nohain's *Vive la France* prohibited by censor. *Marie* appears in book form. Mellerio publishes *La lithographie originale en couleurs*.

1899 participates in important group exhibition at Durand-Ruel's. At about this time enters into agreement with Bernheim-Jeune. Studios: rue Lechapelais and rue Ballu. Roussel settles in l'Etang-la-ville where Bonnard and his wife frequently visit him.

1900 participates in group exhibition at Bernheim-Jeune's. Illustrates *Parallèlement* for Vollard. Begins to live partly in Paris, partly in the country near the city, notably at Montval.

1901 exhibits a large Triptyque at the *Indépendants*. Does vignettes for the *Revue Blanche*. Denis exhibits at the Salon his *Hommage à Cézanne* in which Bonnard is represented.

1902 Vollard publishes *Daphnis et Chloé* with illustrations by Bonnard. Participates in group show at Bernheim-Jeune's. Exhibits a bronze table center piece at Vollard's. Redon draws a lithographic portrait of Bonnard.

1903 exhibits "Portrait of Terrasse" at the *Indépendants;* participates in first *Salon d'Automne* with 3 canvases, among them "Après-midi bourgeoise." Participates in Viennese Secession. Studio: 65 rue de Douai.

1904 one-man show at Bernheim-Jeune's. Sends 3 paintings to the *Indépendants* and 7 to the *Salon d'Automne;* also participates in Impressionist exhibition of *La Libre Esthétique* in Brussels. Draws illustrations for Jules Renard's *Histoires Naturelles*.

1905 exhibits 2 paintings at the *Indépendants* and 5 at the *Salon d'Automne,* where they impress André Gide. At about this time begins to spend summers at Villennes, Vernouillet or Cotteville.

1906 exhibits at the *Indépendants,* the *Salon d'Automne* and the *Secession* in Berlin. Probably one-man show at Bernheim-Jeune's. The Académie Ranson is founded; Bonnard is the only one of the Nabis who avoids teaching there.

1907 participates with 10 paintings in group show at Bernheim-Jeune's; exhibits a decorative panel at the *Salon d'Automne*. Has 2 paintings in French Impressionist exhibition at Prague. 1907-08, shows at Munich *Secession*. Paris studio: 60 rue de Douai in a former convent. Between 1907 and 1911 makes short trips to Belgium, Holland, England, Italy, Spain and Tunisia.

1908 draws illustrations for Mirbeau's *La 628-E-8*. Exhibits 4 paintings at the *Salon d'Automne,* participates in jubilee exhibition of *La Libre Esthétique*.
Sale of the Natanson collection, including 27 paintings by Vuillard and 19 by Bonnard. Bonnard's canvases average 810 francs; 6 bring more than 1000 francs. Among the buyers are Fénéon, Coolus, Bernheim-Jeune, Vuillard (who acquires a "Portrait of Thadée Natanson" of whom he himself had painted several likenesses) and Mirbeau who pays the highest price of the sale,

2050 francs for a painting which, eleven years later, at the Mirbeau sale, was to bring 6000 francs.

1909 in February one-man show at Bernheim-Jeune's with 36 paintings. Exhibits at the *Indépendants* and at *La Libre Esthétique*. Paints portrait of George Besson, 60 rue de Douai. 1909-10, works in Médan.

1910 trip to the south of France early in the year. In March one-man show at Bernheim-Jeune's with 34 paintings. Exhibits 1 painting at the *Indépendants* and 4 decorative panels for Missia Godebska at the *Salon d'Automne* (reproduced in *L'Art Décoratif*). Represented in exhibition of French Art at Leipzig *Kunstverein;* corresponding member of Berlin *Secession*. Paris studios: 60 rue de Douai and 21 quai Voltaire.

1911 May-June, one-man show of work done in 1910-11 at Bernheim-Jeune's, including 27 paintings, a series of drawings and "Mediterranean," 3 decorative panels executed for Morosoff, Moscow. These 3 panels are shown again at the *Salon d'Automne*.

1912 buys *Ma Roulotte*, a small house at Vernonnet near Vernon. From then on until about 1938 divides his time between the Seine Valley and the south (Grasse, St. Tropez, Le Cannet). Exhibits at Paris Triennale, at *La Libre Esthétique* and at the *Salon d'Automne,* for the catalog-cover of which he does a sketch. The two first long articles on Bonnard appear: a "profile" by Thadée Natanson [quoted p. 46-47] and a critical study by Lucie Cousturier. Together with Vuillard, Roussel and Vallotton declines Legion of Honor. Paris studio: 22 rue Tourlaque.

1913 represented by 7 paintings in exhibition of French Art at Zurich Kunsthaus. One-man show in May-June at Bernheim-Jeune's; shows 21 recent works, catalog illustrated with 10 pencil sketches. Contributes sketches to *Cahiers d'Aujourd'hui*. Trip with Vuillard to Holland and England. Shows at *La Libre Esthétique* and at the *Salon d'Automne*. Paris studio: 22 rue Tourlaque.

1914 represented by 5 paintings in exhibition of French 19th Century Art in Copenhagen. Sale of the Roger Marx collection, including 4 early works by Bonnard.
Outbreak of First World War. From 1914-18 Bonnard lives mostly at Saint Germain-en-Laye.

1915 Bonnard is particularly preoccupied with drawing and composition.

1916 represented by 15 paintings in exhibition of French Art in Winterthur, Switzerland.

| 1917 | shows 11 paintings in exhibition of recent works at Bernheim-Jeune's in Oct.-Nov. |

1917   shows 11 paintings in exhibition of recent works at Bernheim-Jeune's in Oct.-Nov.

1918   spends summer in Uriage. Armistice.

1919   Léon Werth publishes the first book on Bonnard. Shows 3 paintings at the *Salon d'Automne*. Paris address: 56 rue Molitor, Auteuil.

1920   shows 1 painting at the *Indépendants*. Between 1920 and 1930 lives only infrequently in Paris.

1921   May-June, one-man show at Bernheim-Jeune's with 24 paintings. Does not show at either *Indépendants* or *Salon d'Automne*. In 1921-22 contributes some sketches to *Cahiers d'Aujourd'hui* edited by George Besson.

1922   represented at Venice Biennale; does not show at either *Indépendants* or *Salon d'Automne*. Bernheim-Jeune publish book on Bonnard by Coquiot.

1923   wins third class medal and $500 award at Carnegie International Exhibition, Pittsburgh. Shows 3 paintings at *Indépendants* and 2 at *Salon d'Automne*. Vollard prints Mirbeau's *Dingo* illustrated with etchings by Bonnard but does not release the book for another four years. Death of Claude Terrasse. Paris address: 56 rue Molitor.

1924   April, large retrospective exhibition, 1891-1922, at Galerie Druet, Paris. June-July, one-man show at Bernheim-Jeune's. Does not send anything to the *Indépendants*.

1925   buys small house at Le Cannet near Cannes. Begins to do watercolors. Shows 1 painting at *Salon d'Automne*. Paris address: 48 Boulevard des Batignolles.

1926   comes to U.S.A. as member of Carnegie International jury. Represented by 2 paintings at Manes Society exhibition in Prague. Has 6 paintings in retrospective of *Indépendants;* does not show at the *Salon d'Automne*. In Nov.-Dec. one-man show of 20 recent paintings at Bernheim-Jeune's.

1927   Vollard releases *Dingo*. Shows 1 painting each at *Indépendants* and *Salon d'Automne*. The painter's nephew, Charles Terrasse, publishes a book on Bonnard.

1928   in April, de Hauke & Co. organize exhibition of 40 paintings by Bonnard in New York; catalog introduction by Claude Anet. Shows 1 painting at *Salon d'Automne*. Paris address: 48 Boulevard des Batignolles.

1929   represented in exhibition of Modern French Art, April-May, Palais des Beaux-Arts, Brussels. Does not show at *Indépendants*. May 16, sale of the collection of Alexandre Natanson, including some of Bonnard's sketches for the *Revue Blanche*.

1930   represented by 7 paintings in Jan.-Feb. exhibition of "Painting in Paris" at Museum of Modern Art, New York. Vollard publishes *La Vie de Sainte Monique,* illustrated by Bonnard. Does not show at *Indépendants*.

1931   between 1930 and 1932 sojourns in Arcachon.

1932   July exhibition of color lithographs by Bonnard and drawings by Sickert at Leicester Gallery, London. Between 1932 and 1938 sojourns repeatedly in Deauville and Trouville.

1933   one-man show at Bernheim-Jeune's in June.

1934   March, exhibition of 44 paintings at Wildenstein Gallery, New York.

1935   Feb.-March, represented in exhibition *Artistes de Paris* at Palais des Beaux-Arts, Brussels. May, Bonnard exhibition at Reid and Lefevre Gallery, London. June, exhibition of Portraits by Bonnard at Galerie Braun & Co., Paris. Institute of Art, Boston: *La Vie Française,* exhibition of paintings chiefly by Bonnard and Vuillard.

1936   wins second prize at Carnegie International Exhibition. Represented in exhibition of *Peintres de la Revue Blanche,* organized by Bolette Natanson in Paris. December, represented by 19 paintings in exhibition of works by Bonnard and Vuillard, Galerie Paul Rosenberg, Paris.

1937   June-October, represented with large group of works at Paris World's Fair, *Les Maîtres de l'Art Indépendant.* 6 paintings in group show at Tooth & Sons, London, May-June.

1938   March-April, represented in group shows at Rosenberg & Helft Gallery, London, and at Durand-Ruel's, Paris, in May-June. December 1938-January 1939, loan exhibition of paintings and prints by Bonnard and Vuillard at Art Institute of Chicago.

1939   February-April, represented at exhibition *Parijsche Schilders* at Municipal Museum, Amsterdam. March, 51 paintings in retrospective at Svensk-Franska Konstgalleriet, Stockholm. Exhibition of works by Bonnard, Laprade, Bouche at Durand-Ruel's in Paris. June, exhibition of 40 pastels, watercolors and drawings by Bonnard and van Dongen at J. Rodrigues-Henriques'. Does not show at the *Indépendants*. Upon outbreak of Second World War, Bonnard remains in Le Cannet; does not return to Paris before 1945.

1940   Defeat of France. Death of Madame Bonnard and of Vuillard.

1941   Sale of part of the Fénéon Collection in Paris; 6 paintings by Bonnard bring close to one million francs. 12 paintings exhibited at Galerie Petridès, Paris.

1942   March, show of Bonnard drawings, watercolors and prints at Weyhe Gallery, New York.

1943   represented by 4 paintings in Bonnard-Vuillard exhibition, Paul Rosenberg and Co., New York.

1944   illustrates a group of early letters for Tériade, editor of *Verve*, published in facsimile under title: *Correspondances. Formes et Couleurs* (Switzerland) and *Le Point* publish special issues devoted to Bonnard.
Liberation of France.

1945   short visit to Paris. Nov.-Dec., exhibition of 40 gouaches, pastels, watercolors and drawings by Bonnard and Marquet at J. Rodrigues-Henriques'. Bonnard writes short introduction for exhibition of work by Stephane Agasse at same gallery.

1946   June-July, retrospective show of 34 major works organized by Bernheim-Jeunes, rue Desbordes-Valmore, Paris. Dec. 1946-Jan. 1947, exhibition of 15 paintings at Bignou Gallery, New York.

Bonnard agrees to project of large retrospective show to be organized by Museum of Modern Art, New York, to celebrate his eightieth birthday in 1947. Prepares with Tériade a special *Verve* issue which he arranges and illustrates. Shows at the *Salon l'Automne*.

1947   January 23, death of Bonnard in Le Cannet.
Feb., exhibition of 13 paintings at Galerie Georges Moos, Zurich. Feb.-March, represented by 2 decorative panels in exhibition *Sur 4 Murs*, Galerie Maeght, Paris. March, the *Indépendants* organize "Hommage à Pierre Bonnard," including 11 paintings. The artist's nephew arranges retrospective exhibitions in Copenhagen, Amsterdam (77 paintings, drawings, etc.). June-July, represented by 16 paintings in exhibition "Bonnard and his French Contemporaries," Lefevre Gallery, London. Sept., exhibition of 34 paintings and 20 lithographs at Svensk-Franska Konstgalleriet, Stockholm. Oct.-Dec., large retrospective exhibition at Paris Orangerie (c. 100 paintings, 27 drawings, watercolors and gouaches, 33 prints, 17 illustrated books).

Catalog to the Exhibition

LENDERS TO THE EXHIBITION

Jean and Henry Bernheim-Dauberville, Paris; Louis Carré, Paris; Ludwig Charell, New York; Mr. and Mrs. Ralph F. Colin, New York; Miss Etta Cone, Baltimore; Henry Decoin, Paris; Mrs. William M. Elkins, Philadelphia; Mrs. John Work Garrett, Baltimore; Mr. and Mrs. Leo Glass, New York; Jean Goriany, Lima, Peru; Marcel Guiot, Paris; Mrs. Hedy Hahnloser-Bühler, Winterthur; Leonard C. Hanna, Jr., Cleveland; Mrs. S. Kaye, England; Dr. and Mrs. David M. Levy, New York; Mr. and Mrs. Sam A. Lewisohn, New York; Jacques Lindon, New York; Wright Ludington, Santa Barbara, Calif.; George Lurcy, New York; Mr. and Mrs. Samuel A. Marx, Chicago; Mrs. Saidie A. May, Baltimore; Captain Edward Molyneux, Paris; Mrs. Duncan Phillips, Washington; Mr. and Mrs. Joseph Pulitzer, Jr., St. Louis; Raoul de Ricci, Paris; Mr. and Mrs. Laurence S. Rockefeller, New York; Jacques Rodrigues-Henriques, Paris; Sam Salz, New York; Mr. and Mrs. James Thrall Soby, Farmington, Conn.; Louis E. Stern, New York; Mr. and Mrs. Charles Terrasse, Fontainebleau; Miss Renée Terrasse, Paris; Benjamin Weiss, New York; E. Weyhe, New York; Georges Wildenstein, New York; Mrs. Emily M. Wilson, Rectortown, Va.

Stedelijk Museum, Amsterdam; The Baltimore Museum of Art; Kunstmuseum, Berne; The Brooklyn Museum, New York; The Art Institute of Chicago; Musée de Grenoble; The Metropolitan Museum of Art, New York; The Spencer Collection, The New York Public Library; Smith College Museum of Art, Northampton, Mass.; Musée d'Art Moderne, Paris; The Springfield Museum of Fine Arts, Springfield, Mass.; The Toledo Museum of Art, Toledo, Ohio; Phillips Memorial Gallery, Washington; Kunstverein, Winterthur, The Worcester Art Museum, Worcester, Mass.

French Art Galleries, Inc., New York; Kleemann Galleries, New York; Pierre Matisse Gallery, New York; Paul Rosenberg and Co., New York; Jacques Seligmann and Co., New York.

PAINTINGS

A star preceding the title indicates that the work is illustrated. Unless otherwise indicated the medium is oil on canvas; height precedes width.

* 1 Study of a Red Partridge, 1889. 8¾ x 6¼″. Lent by Raoul de Ricci, Paris. *Ill. p. 60.*

* 2 Intimacy, c. 1891. 15 x 14¼″. Lent by Charles Terrasse, Fontainebleau. *Ill. p. 62.*

* 3 Screen, c. 1891-92. Four panels, tempera on cloth mounted on wood, 63 x 20″ each. Lent by Louis Carré, courtesy Mrs. Walter Russell Batsell, New York. *Ill. p. 64.*

* 4 The Checkered Blouse, 1892. 24 x 13″. Lent by Charles Terrasse, Fontainebleau. *Ill. p. 63.*

* 5 Street in Eragny (Oise), c. 1894. Oil on wood, 13⅜ x 10¼″. Lent by Captain Edward Molyneux, Paris. *Ill. p. 66.*

* 6 The Cab Horse, Boulevard des Batignolles, c. 1895. Oil on wood, 11¾ x 15¾″. Lent by Captain Edward Molyneux, Paris. *Ill. p. 68.*

* 6a Roofs, c. 1895-1900. 13⅞ x 15⅛″. Lent by Dr. and Mrs. David M. Levy, New York. *Ill. p. 67.*

* 7 At the Moulin Rouge, 1896. 23½ x 16″. Lent by Wright Ludington, Santa Barbara, California. *Ill. p. 69.*

8 The Fortune Teller, c. 1896. Oil on wood, 9½ x 10⅝″. Private collection, Paris.

* 9 The Fair, c. 1898. Oil on cardboard, 13¾ x 10⅝″. Private collection, Paris. *Ill. p. 25.*

* 10 Nude with Raised Arm, 1898. Oil on wood, 16⅛ x 23¼″. Lent by Henry Decoin, Paris. *Ill. p. 70.*

11 Little Girl with Cat (the artist's niece, Renée Terrasse), 1899. 19¾ x 19″. Lent by Miss Renée Terrasse, Paris.

* 12 Luncheon Table, c. 1900. 19½ x 25¾″. Cone Collection, bequest of Frederic W. Cone to The Baltimore Museum of Art. *Ill. p. 71.*

* 13 Street Scene, 1900. 13 x 23″. Lent by French Art Galleries, Inc., New York. *Ill. p. 72.*

* 14 Movement in the Street, 1900. 14 x 19″. Lent by the Phillips Memorial Gallery, Washington, D. C. *Ill. p. 72.*

15 The Desert, 1902. Oil on wood. 13 x 17¼″. Private collection, Paris.

* 16 Portrait of Claude Terrasse, 1902. 37⅜ x 30⅜″. Lent by Charles Terrasse, Fontainebleau. *Ill. p. 41.*

* 17 Bourgeois Afternoon (the Terrasse family at Les Lemps in Dauphiné), 1902-03. 54¾ x 83½″. Private collection Bernheim-Jeune, Paris. *Ill. p. 37.*

* 18 The Boulevard, c. 1904. 32 x 16½″. Lent by Jacques Seligmann and Co., New York. *Ill. p. 78.*

19 The Milliner, c. 1905. Oil on wood, 16⅛ x 13″. Lent by the Kunstverein, Winterthur.

* 20 Portrait of a Woman, c. 1906. Oil on wood, 20 x 16″. Lent by Mr. and Mrs. Leo Glass, New York. *Ill. p. 73.*

* 21 The Lunch, 1906. 24 x 36¼″. Private collection, Paris. *Ill. p. 74.*

* 22 Model in an Armchair, c. 1907. Oil on wood, 24 x 32¼″. Lent by Jacques Lindon, New York. *Ill. p. 76.*

23 Street Covered with Snow, 1908. 13¼ x 18″. Lent by Paul Rosenberg and Co., New York.

* 24 The Loge (Gaston and Josse Bernheim-Jeune and their wives), 1908. 35½ x 47¼″. Private collection, Bernheim-Jeune, Paris. *Ill. p. 75.*

* 25 *La Bouillabaisse,* c. 1910. 24¾ x 12¼″. Lent by Mrs. Hedy Hahnloser-Bühler, Winterthur. *Ill. p. 77.*

* 26 Siesta — The Artist's Studio, c. 1910. 43 x 51½″. Lent by Mrs. S. Kaye through the courtesy of the Lefevre Gallery, London. *Ill. p. 80.*

27 Siesta, c. 1910. 32 x 50″. Private collection, New York.

* 28 The Pont de Grenelle and the Eiffel Tower, c. 1912 (?). 21¼ x 26¾″. Private collection, Paris. *Ill. p. 79.*

* 29 Tugboat on the Seine near Rolleboise, c. 1912 (?). 22 x 31″. Lent by Mrs. John Work Garrett, Baltimore. *Ill. p. 82.*

* 30 In a Southern Garden, 1913. 33 x 44½″. Lent by the Kunstmuseum, Berne. *Ill. p. 81.*

* 31 After the Shower, 1914. 37½ x 26″. Lent by Louis E. Stern, New York. *Color frontispiece.*

* 32 Boating on the Seine (Madame Bonnard), 1915. 22 x 20″. Lent by Sam Salz, New York. *Ill. p. 83.*

* 33 Woman Washing Herself, 1916. 16 x 16⅞″. Private collection Bernheim-Jeune, Paris. *Ill. p. 85.*

33a Rue Tholozé, Montmartre, 1917. 25½ x 13″. Lent by Mr. and Mrs. Ralph F. Colin, New York.

34 Yellow Screen, c. 1917. 53½ x 27½″. Lent by Jacques Seligmann and Co., New York.

* 35 The Source — Kneeling Bather, c. 1917. 32 x 17¼″. Private collection, Paris. *Ill. p. 84.*

* 36 L'Estérel, c. 1917. 22 x 28¾″. Lent by the Stedelijk Museum, Amsterdam. *Ill. p. 86.*

* 37 Abduction of Europa, 1919. 46¼ x 60¼″. Lent by the Toledo Museum of Art, Toledo, Ohio. *Ill. p. 87.*

* 38 Nude in Front of a Fireplace, 1919. 46½ x 19¼″. Lent by the Kunstverein, Winterthur. *Ill. p. 88.*

* 39 Dressing Table and Mirror, c. 1920. 49¼ x 43⅜″. Private collection, Lugano, lent through the courtesy of the Galerie Georges Moos, Geneva-Zurich. *Ill. p. 89.*

40 Still Life with Cat, c. 1920. 45 x 39½″. Lent by George Lurcy, New York.

* 41 Still Life with Petroleum Lamp, 1921. 28⅜ x 34¼″. Private collection, Zurich. *Ill. p. 91.*

* 42 The Open Window, 1921. 46½ x 37¾″. Lent by the Phillips Memorial Gallery, Washington, D. C. *Ill. p. 92.*

* 43 Woman and Dog, 1922. 27 x 15½″. Lent by the Phillips Memorial Gallery, Washington, D. C. *Ill. p. 97.*

* 44 The Riviera — Large Midi Landscape, c. 1923. 31 x 30″. Lent by the Phillips Memorial Gallery, Washington, D. C. *Ill. p. 93.*

* 45 Still Life with Basket of Bananas, 1923. 24 x 25½″. Private collection, Switzerland. *Ill. p. 90.*

46 The Tablecloth, c. 1924. 13¼ x 23⅞″. Lent by Mrs. Duncan Phillips, Washington, D. C.

46a Breakfast in the Garden, c. 1924. 19½ x 16¼″. Lent by the Saidie A. May Collection, the Baltimore Museum of Art.

* 47 *La chevelure d'or,* c. 1924. 26½ x 21″. Private collection, New York. *Ill. p. 101.*

* 48 Portrait of Madame Bonnard, c. 1925. 30½ x 19¾″. Private collection, France. *Ill. p. 96.*

* 49 The Dining Room, 1925. 50½ x 74″. Private collection. *Ill. p. 98.*

* 50 Village Scene, c. 1925-30. 28¾ x 20½″. Anonymous loan through the courtesy of the Worcester Art Museum, Worcester, Massachusetts. *Ill. p. 95.*

51 Saint-Tropez, c. 1925-30. 33 x 34″. Anonymous loan through the courtesy of the Worcester Art Museum, Worcester, Massachusetts.

* 52 The Palm, 1926. 44 x 57½″. Lent by the Phillips Memorial Gallery, Washington, D. C. *Ill. p. 102.*

* 53 Table with Music Album, 1926-32. 48 x 36″. Private collection, New York. *Ill. pp. 50, 103.*

* 54 Luncheon, c. 1927. 16¼ x 24½″. The Museum of Modern Art, New York. Given anonymously. *Reproduced in color p. 99.*

55 Breakfast Room, c. 1927-30. 25⅝ x 39⅝″. Lent by the Brooklyn Museum, New York.

* 56 Strawberries, 1928. 10½ x 10″. Lent by Mrs. Duncan Phillips, Washington, D. C. *Ill. p. 105.*

* 57 The Checkered Dress, 1928. 30⅞ x 18⅝″. Lent by Mr. and Mrs. Laurence S. Rockefeller, New York. *Ill. p. 111.*

58 Grapes, c. 1928. 16½ x 18″. Lent by Mr. and Mrs. James Thrall Soby, Farmington, Connecticut.

59 Woman with Basket of Fruit, c. 1928. 27 x 15″. Cone Collection, bequest of Frederic W. Cone to The Baltimore Museum of Art.

* 60 The Road to Nantes, c. 1930. 26¾ x 25⅝″. Lent by Leonard C. Hanna, Jr., Cleveland. *Ill. p. 104.*

* 61 Landscape of the Midi, c. 1930. 24⅝ x 32″. Lent by the Smith College Museum of Art, Northampton, Massachusetts. *Ill. p. 112.*

* 62 *Le pot provençal*, 1930. 29¾ x 24½″. Lent by Mrs. Hedy Hahnloser-Bühler, Winterthur. *Ill. p. 106.*

* 63 Bowl with Fruit, 1930. 18½ x 12¼″. Private collection, Paris. *Ill. p. 107.*

* 64 Breakfast Room (Arcachon), 1930-31. 63¼ x 44⅛″. The Museum of Modern Art, New York. Given anonymously. *Ill. p. 109.*

64a Still Life in Yellow and Red, Le Cannet, 1931. 18½ x 26¾″. Lent by the Musée de Grenoble.

* 65 Interior with View of Landscape, c. 1930-35. 42⅜ x 25″. Lent by Mr. and Mrs. Sam A. Lewisohn, New York. *Ill. p. 110.*

* 66 *Cabinet de toilette*, 1932. 47¼ x 47¼″. Lent by Mr. and Mrs. Samuel A. Marx, Chicago. *Ill. p. 117.*

*66a White Interior, 1933. 43 x 63¾″. Lent by the Musée de Grenoble. *Ill. p. 114.*

* 67 Dish with Fruit, 1933. 22¾ x 20¾″. Lent by Mrs. William M. Elkins, Philadelphia. *Ill. p. 118.*

* 68 Landscape, 1933. 42⅛ x 24¾″. Lent by the Kunstverein, Winterthur. *Ill. p. 120.*

69 Landscape of the Midi, c. 1935. 39½ x 49½″. Lent by Wright Ludington, Santa Barbara, California.

* 70 Corner of a Table, c. 1935. 65¾ x 64⅜″. Lent by the Musée d'Art Moderne, Paris. *Ill. p. 113.*

* 71 Still Life with Fruit, 1936. 14¼ x 24″. Lent by Mr. and Mrs. Joseph Pulitzer, Jr., St. Louis. *Ill. p. 119.*

* 72 The Mediterranean at Saint-Tropez, 1936. 18 x 22″. Lent by Sam Salz, New York. *Ill. p. 123.*

* 73 The Checkered Tablecloth, 1936. 28½ x 30″. Private collection, New York. *Ill. p. 127.*

* 74 Self Portrait, 1938. 23 x 26⅜″. Lent by Georges Wildenstein, New York. *Reproduced in color p. 121.*

* 75 Nude in a Bathtub, 1938-43. 48⅜ x 59⅞″. Private collection, Paris. *Ill. p. 128.*

* 76 The Harbor of Trouville, 1938-46. 30¼ x 40½″. Lent by the Musée d'Art Moderne, Paris. *Ill. p. 130.*

* 77 Dark Nude, 1943-45. 31⅞ x 25⅝″. Lent by Louis Carré, Paris. *Ill. p. 129.*

78 Landscape with Red Roof (Le Cannet), 1944. 25⅛ x 22½″. Private collection, Paris.

79 The Artist's Garden at Le Cannet, 1944-46. 25⅛ x 21¼″. Lent by Charles Terrasse, Fontainebleau.

* 80 Stiff Ascent at Le Cannet, 1945. 23⅝ x 28¾″. Lent by Louis Carré, Paris. *Ill. p. 133.*

* 81 Circus Horse, 1946. 37 x 46½″. Lent by Charles Terrasse, Fontainebleau. *Reproduced in color p. 131.*

* 82 Flowering Almond-Tree, 1946-47. 17¼ x 15″. Private collection, France. *Ill. p. 134.*

WATERCOLORS AND GOUACHES

* 83 Woman with Dog, c. 1892. Watercolor, 10⅛ x 7¼″. Lent by the Springfield Museum of Fine Arts, Springfield, Massachusetts. *Ill. p. 21.*

83a Seated Nude, c. 1904. Watercolor, 9 x 7⅝″. Lent by E. Weyhe, New York.

84 Open Door, c. 1925 (?). Watercolor, 28½ x 20″. Lent by Mrs. Emily M. Wilson, Rectortown, Virginia.

85 Cloud over the Sea, c. 1930. Gouache, 11 x 14¼″. Lent by Charles Terrasse, Fontainebleau.

* 86 Still Life, 1930-31. Gouache, 6½ x 5⅛″. Private collection, France. *Ill. p. 108.*

87 House among Pine Trees (Arcachon), 1930-31. Gouache, 6¼ x 5⅛″. Private collection, France.

* 88 The French Window (Arcachon), 1930-31. Gouache, 6¼ x 5⅛″. Private collection, France. *Ill. p. 108.*

* 89 Mediterranean, c. 1935 (?). Gouache, 9¾ x 13″. Lent by the Smith College Museum of Art, Northampton, Massachusetts. *Ill. p. 123.*

90 The Harbor of Cannes, c. 1935. Watercolor, 9½ x 12½″. Lent by Pierre Matisse Gallery, New York.

91 The Harbor of Cannes, c. 1938. Watercolor, 10½ x 14½″. Lent by Pierre Matisse Gallery, New York.

* 92 Still Life, Preparation for Lunch, 1940. Gouache, 20¼ x 26″. Lent by the Art Institute of Chicago. *Ill. p. 124.*

DRAWINGS

* 93 The Nursery, c. 1897. Pen and ink, 6½ x 4½". Lent by Marcel Guiot, Paris. *Ill. p. 29.*

94 Standing Nude, c. 1900. Charcoal, 14⅝ x 9". Lent by the Metropolitan Museum of Art, New York.

* 95 Project for the cover of Jules Renard's *Histoires Naturelles,* 1904. Brush and ink, 12 x 7⅞". Lent by E. Weyhe, New York. *Ill. p. 15.*

96 Cover for *Histoires Naturelles,* 1904. Brush and ink, 11¾ x 7⅞". Lent by E. Weyhe, New York.

* 97 Hen, illustration for *Histoires Naturelles* (p. 16), 1904. Brush and ink, 12¼ x 7⅝". Lent by E. Weyhe, New York. *Ill. p. 45.*

98 Rooster, illustration for *Histoires Naturelles* (p. 26), 1904. Brush and ink, 12 x 7¾". Lent by E. Weyhe, New York.

99 Swan, illustration for *Histoires Naturelles* (p. 65), 1904. Brush and ink, 12⅛ x 7½". Lent by E. Weyhe, New York.

*100 Cat, illustration for *Histoires Naturelles* (p. 75), 1904. Brush and ink, 12⅛ x 7⅜". Lent by E. Weyhe, New York. *Ill. p. 45.*

101 Colt, illustration for *Histoires Naturelles* (p. 113), 1904. Brush and ink, 11⅞ x 7⅜". Lent by E. Weyhe, New York.

*102 Goat, illustration for *Histoires Naturelles* (p. 136), 1904. Brush and ink, 12⅛ x 7¾". Lent by E. Weyhe, New York. *Ill. p. 45.*

103 Blackbirds, illustration for *Histoires Naturelles* (p. 286), 1904. Brush and ink, 12⅛ x 7¾". Lent by E. Weyhe, New York.

104 Woman Washing Herself, c. 1920 (?). Pencil, 9⅝ x 6⅛". Private collection, Paris.

105 The Seine at Vernon, c. 1925 (?). Pencil, 9⅞ x 8½". Private collection, Paris.

*106 Self Portrait, c. 1925. Pencil and pen and ink, 5½ x 6¾". Lent by Mrs. Charles Terrasse, Fontainebleau. *Ill. p. 11.*

*107 Still Life of Fruit, c. 1925-30. Pencil, 11¾ x 13¼". Private collection, Zurich. *Ill. p. 54.*

108 Portrait of Isabelle Leconte-Dunouÿ, study for a painting, 1929. Pencil, 9⅞ x 13⅜". Lent by Jacques Rodrigues-Henriques, Paris.

109 Woman Washing Herself, c. 1930 (?). Pencil, 19⅛ x 12¼". Private collection, Paris.

*110 The Model, c. 1938. Pencil, 20½ x 14⅝". Private collection, France. *Ill. p. 55.*

*111 Interior, c. 1938. Pencil, 9⅞ x 12⅝". Private collection, France. *Ill. p. 56.*

112 Mare and Colt Galloping on a Meadow at Deauville, c. 1938. Pencil, 9½ x 12⅝". Private collection, Paris.

113 Nativity, 1944-45. Pencil and pastel, 17⅜ x 21⅝". Private collection, France.

PRINTS

*114 France-Champagne, poster, 1891. Color lithograph, 30¾ x 19¾". Floury No. 1.[1] The Cleveland Museum of Art (The Mr. and Mrs. Lewis B. Williams Collection). *Ill. p. 19.*

Petites Scènes Familières, c. 1893. Illustrations for a Music Album by Claude Terrasse. Lithographs. Floury No. 5. Lent by Jean Goriany through the courtesy of the Brooklyn Museum, New York:

115 *Do, do, l'enfant do.* 6 x 9⅜".
 Quadrille. 4⅜ x 9⅛".

116 *Le dimanche matin à la campagne.* 5¾ x 9".

*117 Family Scene, 1893. Color lithograph, 12⅜ x 7⅛". Floury No. 4. Lent by the Metropolitan Museum of Art, New York. *Ill. p. 21.*

*118 Dogs, 1893. Lithograph, $14\frac{7}{16}$ x 10¼", published in *L'Escarmouche,* December 10, 1893. Floury No. 6. The Museum of Modern Art, New York. Gift of Mrs. John D. Rockefeller, Jr. *Ill. p. 23.*

119 Young Girl with Black Stockings, 1893. Lithograph, $11\frac{7}{16}$ x $5\frac{1}{16}$", published in *L'Escarmouche,* January 14, 1894. Floury No. 8. The Museum of Modern Art, New York. Gift of Mrs. John D. Rockefeller, Jr.

120 *La Revue Blanche,* poster, 1894. Color lithograph, 31½ x 21¼". Floury No. 10. Lent by the Metropolitan Museum of Art, New York.

*121 Cover for an Album of Prints published by *La Revue Blanche,* 1895. Lithograph, $15\frac{11}{16}$ x 11⅜". Floury No. 13. Private collection, New York. *Ill. p. 31.*

Quelques Aspects de la Vie de Paris, 1895, published by A. Vollard. Floury No. 16. 6 from a series of 13 color lithographs:

122 Avenue du Bois. 12⅜ x 18⅛". Lent by the Metropolitan Museum of Art, New York.

*123 Houses on a Court. $13\frac{13}{16}$ x 10¼". Lent by the Metropolitan Museum of Art, New York. *Ill. p. 26.*

[1] *See Jean Floury: Essai de Catalogue de l'oeuvre gravé et lithographié de Pierre Bonnard* in: *Charles Terrasse: Bonnard, Paris, 1927.*

124 Boulevard. 6⅞ x 17⅛″. The Cleveland Museum of Art.

*125 Bridge. 10⅝ x 16⅛″. Lent by the Metropolitan Museum of Art, New York. *Ill. p. 27.*

*126 Vegetable Vendor. 11$\frac{7}{16}$ x 13⅜″. Lent by the Metropolitan Museum of Art, New York. *Ill. p. 28.*

127 Arc de Triomphe. 12⅝ x 18½″. The Museum of Modern Art, New York. Gift of Mrs. Saidie A. May.

128 La Dernière Croisade, c. 1896. Program for the Théâtre de l'Oeuvre (proof printed before the text). Floury No. 22. Lithograph, 11$\frac{13}{16}$ x 19½″. Lent by Kleemann Galleries, New York.

129 Orchard, c. 1896. Color lithograph, 13 x 14$\frac{3}{16}$″. Floury No. 21. Lent by the Brooklyn Museum, New York.

130 *L'Estampe et l'Affiche,* poster, c. 1896. Color lithograph, 31½ x 23⅝″. Floury No. 23. Lent by Ludwig Charell, New York.

*131 Laundry Girl, 1896. Color lithograph, 11$\frac{7}{16}$ x 7⅞″, published by Vollard. Floury No. 25. Lent by the Brooklyn Museum, New York. *Ill. p. 31.*

132 Boating, 1896-97. Color lithograph, 10$\frac{9}{16}$ x 18½″, published by Vollard. Floury No. 27. The Museum of Modern Art, New York. Gift of Mrs. John D. Rockefeller, Jr.

Repertoire du Théâtre des Pantins, 1896-98. Covers for Music sheets published by the *Mercure de France.* Text by Franc-Nohain, music by Terrasse. 2 from a series of 5 lithographs:

133 *Berceuse obscène.* 13¾″ x 10⅝″. Floury No. 29.

134 *Paysage de neige.* 13⅞ x 10⅝″. Floury No. 30. Lent by Benjamin Weiss, New York.

*135 Horse Cab, 1897. Color lithograph for a screen (*see illustration p. 65*). 7$\frac{11}{16}$ x 17¾″. Floury No. 35. The Museum of Modern Art, New York. Gift of Mrs. John D. Rockefeller, Jr. *Ill. p. 17.*

136 At the Theatre, 1898. Frontispiece for Mellerio's *Lithographie originale en couleurs.* Color lithograph, 8¼ x 7½″. Floury No. 38. Lent by the Metropolitan Museum of Art, New York.

*137 Portrait of Ambroise Vollard, c. 1914 (?). Etching, 14 x 9$\frac{7}{16}$″. Floury No. 62. Private collection, New York. *Ill. p. 49.*

138 Portrait of Auguste Renoir, c. 1914. Etching, 10 x 7¾″. Floury No. 63. Lent by Ludwig Charell, New York.

139 In the Street, c. 1920 (?). Color lithograph, 19$\frac{1}{16}$ x 25¾″. Lent by the Art Institute of Chicago (William McCallin McKee Memorial Collection).

140 Woman in a Bathtub, 1924-25. Lithograph, 11¾ x 8¼″. Floury No. 51. The Cleveland Museum of Art.

141 *La Coupe,* 1925. Lithograph, 7⅜ x 10⅛″. Floury No. 51. The Cleveland Museum of Art.

ILLUSTRATED BOOKS

142 Petit Solfège Illustré, Paris, 1893. Music by Charles Terrasse; illustrated with lithographs. Lent by Pierre Bérès, Inc., New York.

*143 Marie, by Peter Nansen, published by La Revue Blanche, Paris, 1898. Illustrated with line cuts after brush and ink drawings. The Museum of Modern Art, New York. *Ill. p. 43.*

*144 Parallèlement, by Paul Verlaine, published by Ambroise Vollard, Paris, 1900. Illustrated with lithographs printed in rose and blue. Lent by the Spencer Collection, the New York Public Library. *Ill. p. 32.*

*145 Daphnis et Chloé, by Longus, published by Ambroise Vollard, Paris, 1902. Illustrated with lithographs. The Museum of Modern Art, New York. Gift of Mrs. John D. Rockefeller, Jr. *Ill. p. 33.*

*146 Histoires Naturelles, by Jules Renard, published by Flammarion, Paris, no date (c. 1906). Illustrated with line cuts after brush and ink drawings. The Museum of Modern Art, New York. *Ill. p. 45.*

*147 Dingo, by Octave Mirbeau, published by Ambroise Vollard, Paris, 1923, released 1927. Illustrated with etchings. Lent by the Metropolitan Museum of Art, New York. *Ill. p. 49.*

143

Bibliography

The following references are arranged alphabetically by author or title, with publications by institutions filed under the name of the city in which the museum or gallery is located. Materials considered of secondary value, but accessible through the Art Index, the Répertoire d'Art et d'Archéologie as well as standard bibliographies, have not been noted below.

BERNARD KARPEL

ABBREVIATIONS

*This item is in the collection of the Museum of Modern Art Library, Ag *August,* Ap *April,* Aufl *Auflage,* col *colored,* D *December,* ed *edition,* F *February,* Hft *Heft,* il *illustration(s)*, incl *including,* Ja *January,* Je *June,* Jy *July,* Mr *March,* My *May,* N *November,* no *number(s)*, O *October,* p *page(s)*, pl *plate(s)*, por *portrait(s)*, pseud *pseudonym,* S *September,* v *volume(s)*.

TYPICAL ENTRY

BAZIN, GERMAIN. Bonnard. 11il L'Amour de l'Art 14no4:83-9 Ap 1933.

EXPLANATION

An article by Germain Bazin titled Bonnard, containing 11 illustrations, will be found in L'Amour de l'Art, volume 14, number 4, pages 83 to 89 inclusive, in the issue dated April 1933.

* 1 AMSTERDAM. STEDELIJK MUSEUM. Pierre Bonnard . . . juni-juli 1947. 11p plus 7pl 1947.
    Catalog of exhibition of 76 works, including book illustrations and Vuillard's portrait of the artist. Includes essay by Claude Roger-Marx (bibl 154).

 2 ANET, CLAUDE. Pierre Bonnard. p[3-6] *In* De Hauke & Co., New York. Bonnard, April 6th to April 28th. 1928.
    Preface to exhibition catalog.

* 3 ANTHOLOGIE DU LIVRE ILLUSTRÉ PAR LES PEINTRES ET SCULPTEURS DE L'ECOLE DE PARIS. Avant-propos de Claude Roger-Marx . . . Catalogue établi par Albert Skira. pxi,xvi,xviii, 6-10 5il Genève, Editions Albert Skira, 1946.

 4 AURIER, G. ALBERT. Les symbolistes. 2il Revue Encyclopédique 2no32:475-86 Ap 1 1892.

* 5 LES BALLETS SUÉDOIS DANS L'ART CONTEMPORAIN. p40,129,131-2 plus 2pl(1col) Paris, Editions du Trianon, 1931.
    Décor for *Jeux.* Color reproduction in supplementary plates.

* 6 BARNES, ALBERT COOMBS. The art in painting. p334-5 New York, Harcourt, Brace and co., 1937.
    Originally published by the Barnes foundation press, 1925.

* 7 BARAZETTI-DEMOULIN, SUZANNE. Maurice Denis. p28-33 Paris, Editions Bernard Grasset, 1945.

* 7a BARR, ALFRED H. JR. What is modern painting? 3d ed p21 1il New York, The Museum of Modern Art, 1946.

* 8 BASLER, ADOLPHE & KUNSTLER, CHARLES. Le dessin et la gravure modernes en France. p78-80,82,174, 208 2il Paris, G. Crès & cie., 1930.

* 9 ——— Modern French painting: the post-impressionists from Monet to Bonnard. p52-6 et passim 4il New York, W. F. Payson [1931].

* 10 BAZAINE, JEAN. Bonnard et la réalité. 6il(1col) Formes et Couleurs 6no2:39-48 1944.

* 11 BAZIN, GERMAIN. Bonnard. 11il L'Amour de l'Art 14no4:83-9 Ap 1933.
    Accompanied by "notice" by Sterling, p89(bibl 174). Partly reprinted in bibl 197.
    ——— See also bibl 87.

* 12 BEER, FRANÇOIS-JOACHIM. Bonnard. 2il(por) Arts no7:1 Je 21 1946.
    Review of exhibit at MM. Bernheim-Jeunes.
    ——— Eléments d'une fête. See bibl 18.

* 13 ——— Evocation de Pierre Bonnard. 6il(por) Arts de France. no11-12.19-25 1947.

* 14 ——— Fragment des notes sur l'art de Bonnard. Arts no100:3 Ja 3 1947.

* 15 ——— Pierre Bonnard, par François-Joachim Beer, suivi d'un texte de Louis Gillet . . . Préface par Raymond Cogniat. 163p incl 167pl (24col) Marseille, Editions Françaises d'art, 1947.

* 16 BELL, CLIVE. Since Cézanne. 1il p98-104 London, Chatto and Windus, 1922.

* 17 BERNHEIM-JEUNE, JOSEPH & GASTON. L'art moderne, et quelques aspects de l'art d'autrefois . . . d'après la collection privée de MM. J. et G. Bernheim-Jeune. Poèmes de Henri de Régnier. v1:7-10 3il Paris, Bernheim-Jeune, 1919.
Includes poem by Régnier, appreciations by Lucie Cousturier, Thadée Natanson, Octave Mirbeau, Elie Faure. [Edited by Félix Fénéon].

18 BERNHEIM-JEUNE & CIE., PARIS. XXXIV Peintures de Pierre Bonnard . . . 15 juin — 13 juillet. 5il(por) [14]p incl pl 1946.
Catalog with list of 34 works, and introduction *Eléments d'une fête* by François-Joachim Beer.

* 19 BESSON, GEORGE. Aspects de la peinture contemporaine. 1il Le Point 1no2:12-14 Mr 1936.

* 20 ——— Bonnard. [12]p 60il Paris, Braun & cie., 1934 (Collection des maîtres) .

21 ——— Bonnard le solitaire. Silhouette Ap-My 1947.

* 22 ——— 1900-1940, préface de George Besson. p[2,4,5,9] 2il (1col) Lyon, Braun & cie., 1942 (Couleurs des maîtres) .

* 23 ——— Signalements: Pierre Bonnard. 3il(por) Arts de France no4:7-12 Mr 1946.

23a BIDOU, HENRY. Le Salon d'automne. 1il Gazette des Beaux-Arts no641:377-8 N 1910.

24 BLOMBERG, ERIK. Pierre Bonnard. 9il Konstrevy [no1]:1-6 1939.

* 25 BOERS, FRANS. Bij de dood van Bonnard. Kroniek van Kunst und Kultur 8no3:96 1947.

* 26 BONNARD, PIERRE. Correspondances. 89p incl 28pl Paris, Tériade, 1944.

* 27 ——— [Témoignage] p46 *In* Maillol. Paris, Les Amis de l'art, 1946 (Cahier des amis de l'art, no. 10) .
——— See also bibl 89, 128.

* 28 [Bonnard] 7il (4col) Verve 1no3:61-7 incl il O-D 1938.
Illustrations with brief text, including portraits by Rogi André. Cover by Bonnard.

* 29 Bonnard est mort; hommage à Bonnard. Arts no104:1,3 Ja 31 1947.

Contributions by Jacques de Laprade, René Brimo, Claude Roger-Marx, Marcel Zahar, Raymond Cogniat, Pierre Descargues, Michel Florisoone.

* 30 BULLIET, CLARENCE JOSEPH. The significant moderns and their pictures. p126-7 New York, Covici-Friede, 1936.

* 31 CASSOU, JEAN. Bonnard. 19il Arts et Métiers Graphiques no46:9-18 Ap 15 1935.

* 32 ——— Bonnard. Art News 46no3:52 My 1947.

* 33 ——— The lyricism of Bonnard. 9il (1col) Formes no9:4-5 plus il N 1930.
Additional notes, p2.

34 CHARPENTIER, ALBERT. Bonnard, Laprade, Bouche. 15p [Paris, Galeries Durand-Ruel] 1939.
Lettered on cover: Exposition de tableaux, Bonnard, Laprade, Bouche. No catalog of paintings included. *Bonnard* p1-6, partly reprinted in bibl 35.

35 ——— Trois peintres. 2il Prométhée 20no5:177-8 Je 1939.

* 36 CHENEY, SHELDON. The story of modern art. p489-90 New York, Viking press, 1941.

* 37 CHICAGO. ART INSTITUTE. Loan exhibition of paintings and prints by Pierre Bonnard and Edouard Vuillard . . . December 15, 1938 to January 15, 1939. 4il [1938]
Exhibition catalog with essay by Daniel Catton Rich *Bonnard and Vuillard* p[1-4], by Dorothy Stanton *The Lithographs of Bonnard and Vuillard* p[5-6], biographical notes, p[7]. The exhibition is also discussed in the museum Bulletin 32:102-3 D 1938.

38 Clément-Janin, Noël. Essai sur la bibliographie contemporaine de 1900 à 1928. 2il v1:23,36,48,201 Paris, René Kieffer, 1931.

39 COGNIAT, RAYMOND. Autour de Matisse et de Bonnard. L'Amour de l'Art 14no5:117-21 My 1933.
"Tous les peintres dont l'art se rattache directement à l'un ou à l'autre."
——— See also bibl 15.

40 COLOMBIER, PIERRE DU. Douze tableaux de Pierre Bonnard. 4il Beaux-Arts no24:1,7 1941.
At the Galerie Petridès.

* 41 COPENHAGEN, Ny CARLSBERG GLYPTOTEK. Bonnard, udstilling i anledning af Glyptoteket 50-aars jubilaeum maj 1947.
Catalog lists 70 works including Vuillard's portrait of the artist. Preface by Haavard Rostrup.

* 42 COQUIOT, GUSTAVE. Bonnard. 46il (1col) 60p plus pl Paris, Editions Bernheim-Jeune, 1922.

Color plate mounted on cover. Also issued in édition de luxe.

* 43 ——— Cubistes, futuristes, passéistes; essai sur la jeune peinture et la jeune sculpture. 3. éd. p8-12 1il Paris, Librairie Ollendorf, 1914.

* 44 ——— Les indépendants, 1884-1920. 4. éd. p78-9 1il Paris, Librairie Ollendorf [1920].

* 45 COURTHION, PIERRE. Bonnard, peintre du merveilleux. 167p 16il (4col) Lausanne, Marguerat, 1945.

  46 COUSTURIER, LUCIE. Pierre Bonnard. 17il L'Art Décoratif 28:361-76 D 20 1912.
      Extract published in Bernheim-Jeune (bibl 17).

* 47 DEGAND, LÉON, Le vrai Bonnard. Artes 1no7:14-16 Mr 1947.

  48 DENIS, MAURICE. L'époque du symbolisme. 1il Gazette des Beaux-Arts 76:172,176,178 Mr 1934.

* 49 ——— Nouvelles théories, sur l'art moderne, sur l'art sacré, 1914-1921. Paris, L. Rouart et J. Watelin, 1922.

* 50 ——— Théories, 1890-1910, du symbolisme et de Gauguin vers un nouvel ordre classique. 3. éd. Paris, Bibliothèque de l'Occident, 1913.

* 51 DIEHL, GASTON. Hommage à Maillol et Bonnard. 3il (por) Art Présent no1:[38-9] [Jy 1946].

     ——— See also bibl 144.

  52 DORIVAL, BERNARD. Les étapes de la peinture française contemporaine. v1:121-9,169-79 et passim Paris, Gallimard, 1946.

* 53 ——— Images de la peinture française contemporaine; préface et descriptions commentées par Bernard Dorival. p35-6 1il (col) Paris, Editions Nomis [1947?].

* 54 ——— Musée d'art moderne, I — Nabis et cubistes. 1il Bulletin des Musées de France 12no5:10-11 My-Je 1947.

* 55 ——— La peinture française. v2:116-17, [133] Paris, Librairie Larousse, 1942.

  56 ——— Pierre Bonnard. 1il Les Nouvelles Littéraires no1017:1 Ja 30 1947.

*56a ECKSTEIN, HANS. Pierre Bonnard. 11il Prisma 1hft6:30-2 Ap 1947.

* 57 ESCHOLIER, RAYMOND. La peinture française, XXe siècle. 6il (1col) p22-6 Paris, Librairie Floury, 1937.

*57a ESTIENNE, CHARLES. Pierre Bonnard au Musée de l'Orangerie. 2il Arts no136:8 O 17 1947.

* 58 FABRE, F. On dit que Pierre Bonnard est mort. Masques 2no8:[8] 1947.

* 59 FAGE, ANDRÉ. Le collectionneur de peintures modernes. p55,58,80,85,125,152,223-5,252 et passim 1il Paris, Editions Pittoresques, 1930.

  60 FAGUS. L'art de demain. La Revue Blanche 29:542-6 D 1 1902.

*60a FAURE, ELIE. A propos d'une exposition Pierre Bonnard. Cahiers d'Aujourd'hui no5:263-6 Je 1913.

* 61 ——— Histoire de l'art: l'art moderne. p435-6, 438-40,442,444 et passim 3il Paris, G. Crès & cie., 1921.
      Vol. 4 of the Histoire, also issued in an English translation by Walter Pach, New York and London, Harper and brothers, 1924.

*61a ——— Pour remercier Bonnard, Vuillard, Vallotton, Roussel, d'avoir refusé la croix. Cahiers d'Aujourd'hui no2:78-81 D 1912.

     FLOURY, JEAN. Essai de catalogue de l'oeuvre gravé et lithographié de Pierre Bonnard. p187-99 See bibl 176.

  61b FONTAINAS, ANDRÉ. Art moderne. Le Mercure de France 26no101:596-604 My 1898, 34no125:540-7 My 1900.

* 62 ——— Bonnard; 24 phototypies, notice d'André Fontainas. [4]p plus pl Paris Librairie de France [1928] (Les albums d'art Druet. 20).

* 63 ——— Bonnard. v1:155-61 7il (por) In Edouard-Joseph, René. Dictionnaire biographique des artistes contemporains, 1910-1930. Paris, Art & Edition, 1930.

  64 ——— Histoire de la peinture française au XIXe et XXe siècles (1801-1920). Nouv. éd. rev. p278-9, 302,304,315 Paris, Mercure de France, 1922.
      First edition, 1906.

     FORMES ET COULEURS. [Bonnard number] See bibl 67,102,105,177.

  65 FOSCA, FRANÇOIS. Bonnard. 25il 64p Genève, L'Eventail, Librairie Kundig, 1919. (Peintres et sculpteurs d'aujourd'hui. 1).
      Also issued under imprint of Crès, Paris.

  66 ——— Pierre Bonnard. 11il (1col) Art et Décoration 38:65-74 S 1920.

* 67 FUMET, STANISLAS. Bonnard comme expression française de la peinture. 8il (1col) Formes et Couleurs 6no2:13-26 1944.

* 68 GAUTHIER, MAXIMILIEN. Notices bio-bibliographiques des peintres figurant à l'exposition de l'Art vivant: Pierre Bonnard. L'Art Vivant 6no130:392 My 15 1930.

  69 GEFFROY, GUSTAVE. Pierre Bonnard. Le Journal Ja 8 1892.

* 70 GEORGE, WALDEMAR. Bonnard et la douceur de vivre. 4il Formes no33:380-1 1933.
Also published in the English edition.

* 71 ——— Exposition des peintres de la Revue Blanche. 1il L'Amour de l'Art 17no7:267-8 Jy 1936.

72 ——— Pierre Bonnard and the impressionists. 6il Drawing and Design 3no14:48-56 Ag 1927.

73 ——— Pierre Bonnard et l'antique. 4il L'Art et les Artistes 31no162:85-8 D 1935.
Illustrations from "Vie de Sainte Monique."

74 GIDE, ANDRÉ. Promenade au salon d'automne. 1il Gazette des Beaux-Arts no582:481-2 D 1 1905.

* 75 GOLDWATER, ROBERT J. L'Affiche moderne, a revival of poster art after 1880. 2il Gazette des Beaux-Arts 22:174,180-2 D 1942.

* 76 ———Symbolist art and theater: Vuillard, Bonnard, Maurice Denis. 1il Magazine of Art 39no8:366,370 D 1946.

* 77 GORDON, JAN. Modern French painters. p65,87-8, 125 New York, Dodd, Mead and co., 1923.

* 78 GRAUTOFF, OTTO. Bonnard. v4:304 In Thieme, Ulrich & Becker, Felix. Allgemeines Lexikon der bildenden Künstler. Leipzig, Verlag von Wilhelm Engelmann, 1910.
Brief bibliography.

* 79 GREENBERG, CLEMENT. [Bonnard] The Nation 164no2:53 Ja 11 1947.

* 80 GUÉGUEN, PIERRE. Bonnard l'enchanteur. 5il XXe Siècle no2:3-8 My-Je 1938.

81 GUENNE, JACQUES. Bonnard, ou le bonheur de vivre. 5il L'Art Vivant no176:373-5 S 1933.

82 GUTMAN, WALTER. Pierre Bonnard. 3il Art in America 16no5:218-23 Ag 1928.

82a HAHNLOSER-BÜHLER, HEDY. Félix Vallotton et ses amis. Paris, Editions A. Sedrowski, 1936.

83 HEILBUT, E. Lithographien von P. Bonnard. 12il Kunst und Künstler 4:210-24 1906.

* 84 HOEFLIGER, ALFRED. Bonnard und Maillol als Illustratoren von "Daphnis und Chloe." il Werk 34no6:193-7 Je 1947.

* 85 Hommage à Pierre Bonnard. 1il (col) Art et Industrie 7:37 1947.

86 HOPPE, RAGNAR. Pierre Bonnard 6il p184-92 In his: Städer och Konstnärer, resebrev och essäer om konst. Stockholm, Albert Bonniersförlag, 1931.

* 87 HUYGHE, RENÉ. La peinture française: les contemporains. 5il (1col) p18-21,23-5,61 Paris, Editions Pierre Tisné, 1939.
Includes biographical summary by Germain Bazin (supplement).

88 JACOBSEN, GEORG. Bonnard. 14il Kunst og Kultur 25no2:83-102 1939.

* 89 JAKOVSKI, ANATOLE. Interviews et opinions: Bonnard. 5il (por) Arts de France no11-12:27-31 1947.
Includes statements by the artist.

90 JARRY, ALFRED. Paul Verlaine Parallèlement, illustré par Pierre Bonnard. La Revue Blanche 24:317 1901.

90a JEAN, RENÉ. Le Salon d'automne. Gazette des Beaux-Arts no653:378 N 1911.

91 JEDLICKA, GOTTHARD. Pierre Bonnard. 3il Kunst und Künstler 31:444-50 D 1932.

* 92 ——— Pierre Bonnard. Werk 34hft3:25 Mr 1947.

* 93 JEWELL, EDWARD ALDEN. French impressionists and their contemporaries represented in American collections. 4il (1col) p20,22 New York, Hyperion press [&] Random house, 1944.

* 94 JOHNSON, UNA E. Ambroise Vollard, éditeur, 1867-1939; an appreciation and catalogue 2il p12-13,19-20,39,58-66 et passim New York, Wittenborn and co., 1944.

* 95 JOURDAIN, FRANCIS. Pierre Bonnard, ou les vertus de la liberté. 16il (col) 9p plus pl Genève, A. Skira, 1946. (Les trésors de la peinture française).

96 ——— Sagesse de Bonnard. 1il Arts no135:1,5 O 10 1947.

* 97 KLINGSOR, TRISTAN. L'art français depuis vingt ans: la peinture. 1il p54-7 Paris, Editions Rieder, 1928 (c1921).

* 98 ——— Pierre Bonnard. 5il L'Amour de l'Art 2no8:241-6 Ag 1921.

* 99 KOBER, JACQUES. Bonnard et les écoles. L'Arche 6no24:38-41 F 1941.
Also published in Las Moradas 1il 1no2:145-7 Jy-Ag 1947.

*100 ——— Hommage. 1il (por) Derrière le Miroir (Galerie Maeght, Paris) p4-5,8 F-Mr 1947.

*100a LAMOTTE, ANGÈLE. Le bouquet de roses; propos de Pierre Bonnard recueillis en 1943. Verve 5no17-18: [73,75] Ag 1947.

*101 LAPRADE, JACQUES DE. Bonnard. 36il (25col) [14]p plus pl Lyon, Braun et cie. [1944] (Couleurs des maîtres).

*102 ——— Gravures, illustrations, dessins de Pierre Bonnard. 10il (1col) Formes et Couleurs 6no2:50-62 incl pl 1944.

*103 LASSAIGNE, JACQUES. Bonnard et Chagall. 3il (por) Revue de la Pensée Française 7no1:53-7 Ja 1948.

*104 LEYMARIE, JEAN. Présence de Bonnard. 5il (1col, por) L'Amour de l'Art 26no9:264-6 1946.

*105 Lhote, André. Bonnard. 6il (1col) Formes et Couleurs 6no2:3-10 1944.

*106 ——— Bonnard, seize peintures, 1939-1943; introduction de André Lhote. 7p plus 16col pl Paris, Editions du Chêne, 1944.

107 Lugné-Poë, Alexandre. La parade: I, Le sot du Tremplin.-II, Acrobaties, souvenirs et impressions de théâtre, 1894-1902. Paris, Nouvelle revue française, 1930-32.

108 Mahé, Raymond. Bibliographie des livres de luxe de 1900 à 1928. 4v. Paris, René Kieffer, 1931-43.
Supplement, v4: Les artistes illustrateurs.

*109 Maindron, Ernest. Les affiches illustrées (1889-1895). 2il p40-1 Paris, G. Boudet, 1896.

110 Les Maitres de l'Affiche. v1:p138 (col) Paris, L'Imprimerie Chaix, 1896.
La Revue Blanche (1894) also reproduced in McKnight Kauffer, E. The art of the poster. facing p112 New York, Albert & Charles Boni, 1928.

*111 Les Maitres de l'Art Indépendant 1895-1937. 2il (por) p60-1 Paris, Editions Arts et Métiers Graphiques, 1937.
Catalog of exhibition at the Petit Palais, Je-O 1937, lists 33 works by Bonnard and brief data.

112 Marois, Pierre. Des goûts et des couleurs. 185p Paris, Albin Michel, 1947.

113 Marx, R. L'art décoratif et les "symbolistes." Le Voltaire Ag 23 1892.

114 ——— Les indépendants. Le Voltaire Mr 28 1893.

115 ——— [Exhibition review] Le Voltaire O 1 1892.

*116 Mauclair, Camille. Les états de la peinture française de 1850 à 1920. p108,144,150-1 Paris, Payot & cie., 1921.

*117 Mauny, Jacques. Paris letter. 1il The Arts 13no1:51 Ja 1928.

118 Mellerio, André. L'estampe en 1896. 1il L'Estampe et l'Affiche 1:1,5 1897.

119 ——— Exposition: les éditions Vollard. L'Estampe et l'Affiche 3:98-9 1899.

120 ——— La lithographie originale en couleurs. Couverture et estampe de Pierre Bonnard. p9-10 et passim col front Paris, L'Estampe et l'Affiche, 1898.

*121 ——— Le mouvement idéaliste en peinture. p44,50-1 Paris, H. Floury, 1896.

*122 Meier-Graefe, Julius. Bonnard. 4il Ganymed 5:89-104 1925.

*123 ——— Bonnard. 4il Art News 37no14:8-9 D 31 1938.
Commentary occasioned by the Bonnard summer exhibitions in 1933 at Braun and Bernheim-Jeunes, Paris.

*124 ——— Entwicklungsgeschichte der modernen Kunst. 2Aufl. 7il v3:528-39 et passim München, R. Piper & co., Verlag, c1915.
First published in 1904; condensed English translation issued 1908 (bibl 125).

*125 ——— Modern art, being a contribution to a new system of aesthetics. From the German by Florence Simmonds and George W. Chrystal. 2il v1:271-5 et passim New York, G. P. Putnam's sons; London, William Heinemann, 1908.

*126 Morand, Pierre. Pierre Bonnard. 10il Le Courrier Graphique 6no30:3-10 Mr-Ap 1947.

*127 Moro, Cesar. Homenaje a Bonnard [poem] 1il (por) Las Moradas 1no2:143-4 Jy-Ag 1947.

128 Murailles: opinions des artistes et des critiques sur les concours d'affiche. L'Estampe et l'Affiche 2:87 1898.
Quotes brief statement by Bonnard.

129 Natanson, Thadée. A l'Orangerie, Bonnard le magicien. 1il Opéra 4no125:1,6 O 8 1947.

130 ——— Bonnard. Carrefour Ja 23 1947.

131 ——— Des peintres intelligents. La Revue Blanche 22:53-6 My 1 1900.

132 ——— IXe exposition de la Société des artistes indépendants. La Revue Blanche 4:139-46 Ap 1893.

133 ——— Peints à leur tour. Paris, Albin Michel [to be published 1948].

134 ——— Petite gazette d'art. La Revue Blanche 15:213,614 F 1898.

135 ——— Pierre Bonnard. La Revue Blanche 10:71-4 Ja 15 1896.

136 ——— Pierre Bonnard. La Vie Je 15 1912.

*137 ——— Sur une exposition des peintres de la Revue Blanche. 3il Arts et Métiers Graphiques no54:9-18 Ag 15 1936.

——— Un Bonnard que je sais. See bibl 144.

138 ——— Une date de l'histoire de la peinture française. La Revue Blanche 18:504-12 Ap 1 1899.

*139 New York. Museum of Modern Art. Painting in Paris, from American collections, January 19 to February 16 1930. 3il p12,19 New York, The Museum, 1930.
Foreword by Alfred H. Barr, Jr. Lists 7 works by Bonnard with brief note on the artist.

*140 ——— Modern painters and sculptors as illustrators, by Monroe Wheeler. 3il p11,17-18,32-3,98,116-17. New York, Museum of Modern Art, distributed by Simon and Schuster, 1947.

Third revision (1946) of catalog originally issued 1936 to accompany an exhibition of the same title. Bibliography.

*141 PARIS. MUSÉE DE L'ORANGERIE. Exposition Bonnard, octobre-novembre 1947: catalogue. 9il 24p Paris, Editions des musée nationaux, 1947.

Preface by Charles Terrasse. Lists of paintings, gouaches, and watercolors, drawings, prints, illustrated books, and chronology.

*142 PHILLIPS, DUNCAN. The artist sees differently; essays based upon the philosophy of a collection in the making. 10il (1col) p17,53,84-5,125-8,136 et passim New York, E. Weyhe; Washington, D. C. Phillips Memorial Gallery, 1931.

V.1:Text.-2. Plates. "The text of this book is made up of editorials from *Art and Understanding . . .* and essays written for special purposes . . ." Nos. 1-2 of *Art and Understanding* Nov 1929-Mar 1930 have Bonnard illustrations, and references on p63,143-4,172.

*143 ——— A collection in the making, together with brief estimates of the painters in the Phillips memorial gallery. 2il p52-3 Washington, D. C., E. Weyhe [for the] Phillips Memorial Gallery, 1926.

*144 PIERRE BONNARD. 21il (5col,por) 36p Paris, Les Publications Techniques et Artistiques, 1945.

Contents: Léon Werth, Le peintre, p3-18.-Thadée Natanson, Un Bonnard que je sais, p19-26.-Léon Gischia, Leçon de Bonnard, p27-32.-Gaston Diehl, Avec Bonnard, dans la féerie du quotidien, p33-6.

*145 Pierre Bonnard. 27il (1col) L'Art d'Aujourd'hui 4:21-7 plus pl 41-58 Summer 1927.

*145a PISSARO, CAMILLE. Letters to his son Lucien. New York, Pantheon books, 1943.

*146 LE POINT. Bonnard. il 48p Lanzac [Pierre Betz] 1943.

Special number, Le Point, 4no24 1943. Contents: Maurice Denis, Pierre Bonnard, p4-5.-René-Marie, Bonnard et son époque, p6-39.-George Besson, Lettre à Pierre Betz, p40-6.-Charles Terrasse, La porte entr'ouverte, p46-8.

*147 POUTERMAN, J. E. Les livres d'Ambroise Vollard. 4il Arts et Métiers Graphiques no64:45-56 S 15 1938.

Includes checklist of Bonnard editions.

*148 PUY, MICHEL. L'effort des peintres modernes. p94,98-100 Paris, Albert Messein, 1933 (Collection La Phalange).

149 RAYNAL, MAURICE. Peintres du XXe siècle. 4il (3col) p11-13 Genève, Editions d'art Albert Skira, 1947.

*150 REWALD, JOHN. For Pierre Bonnard on his seventy-fifth birthday. 8il (1col) Art News 41:22-5 O 1 1942.

RICH, DANIEL CATTON. Bonnard and Vuillard. See bibl 37.

151 ROGER-MARX, CLAUDE. Bonnard. Revue Occident 1947.

152 ——— Bonnard, illustrateur de La Fontaine. 13il Le Portique no5:42-50 1947.

153 ——— Bonnard, illustrateur et lithographe. 7il Art et Décoration 43:115-20 1923.

*154 ——— Bonnard of het opgetogen oog. 5il Maandblad voor Bildende Kunste 23no3:49-54 Mr 1947.

Originally published as "Bonnard ou l'oeil émerveillé." Europe Nouvelle Je 23 1933. Reprinted in bibl 1.

155 ——— Les dessins de Bonnard. Arts no104:3 Ja 31 1947.

*156 ——— French original engravings from Manet to the present time. 4il (2col) p51-2 London, Paris, New York, Hyperion press, 1939.

Also published as: La gravure originale en France de Manet à nos jours (1939).

157 ——— Un grand peintre est mort. Figaro Littéraire F 1 1947.

158 ——— Les illustrations de Bonnard. 6il Plaisir de Bibliophile 2no5:1-10 Winter 1926.

"Ouvrages illustrés par Bonnard," p11.

*159 ——— Lettre à un jeune peintre. 2il Style en France no5:13-15 Ap 15 1947.

160 ——— L'oeuvre gravé de Pierre Bonnard. 7il L'Art Vivant no145:2-5 incl il F 1931.

*161 ——— Pierre Bonnard, trente reproductions de peintures et dessins précédées d'une étude critique par Claude Roger-Marx. 30il (por) 15p plus pl Paris, Editions de la Nouvelle Française, 1924. (Les peintres français nouveaux, no.19).

Includes brief list of exhibitions, posters, illustrated books, bibliography.

*162 ——— Pierre Bonnard, étude par Claude Roger-Marx, lettre-préface de Tristan Bernard, portrait par Odilon Redon. 46il (por) 24p plus pl Paris, Henry Babou, 1931. (Les artistes du livre, 19).

50 copies on Japan issued, each containing unpublished drawings.

*163 ——— Pierre Bonnard, painter, illustrator and portrayer of the elements of Parisian middle class life. 4il Creative Art 7:112-15 Ag 1930.

Also published in Studio p112-15 1930.

*164 ——— La sainteté de Bonnard. no53:1 Arts F 1
1946.

*165 ——— Vuillard et son temps. p14-17,24,27 et passim
Paris, Editions Arts et Métiers Graphiques, 1945.

*166 RUBOW, JØRN. Pierre Bonnard, apropos en udstil-
ling. 6il Konstrevy 23hft3:124-5 1947.
  Exhibition at the Ny Carlsberg Glyptotek, Mr
  1947.

*167 RUTTER, FRANK. Modern masterpieces, an outline
of modern art. 1il p170-3 London, George Newnes
ltd. [1940].

168. RYDBECK, INGRID. Hos Bonnard i Deauville. 5il
(2por) Konstrevy 13no4:119-23 1937.

*169 SAN LAZZARO, G. DI. Cinquant'anni de pittura
moderna en Francia. 1il p43-6 Roma, Danesi,
1945.

170 SENTENAC, PAUL. Les décors français des ballets
suédois. 1il Renaissance 4no1:24-30 Ja 1921.

171 ——— Deux créateurs d'harmonie, Aristide Maillol
et Pierre Bonnard. 3il Mobilier et Décoration
26no4:39-44 O 1946.

172 SÉRUSIER, PAUL. A B C de la peinture, suivi d'une
étude sur la vie et l'oeuvre de Paul Sérusier par
Maurice Denis. Paris, Floury, 1942.

172a SIGNAC, PAUL. Fragments du journal de Paul
Signac. il Arts de France no17-18:75-82 1947.

172b ——— Les besoins individuels et la peinture. Encyclopédie Française [v16:chapter 2] Paris, 1935.

  SKIRA, ALBERT. See bibl 3.

  STANTON, DOROTHY. The lithographs of Bonnard
  and Vuillard. See bibl 37.

*173 STENSTADVOLD, HALCON. Pierre Bonnard og hans
tid. 8il Bonytt 7no7-8:136-40 1947.

*174 STERLING, CHARLES. Bonnard [notice biographique
et bibliographique] L'Amour de L'Art 14no4:89
Ap 1933.

*175 STOCKHOLM. SVENSK-FRANSKA KONSTGALLERIET. Pi-
erre Bonnard (1867-1947) i svensk ägo September,
1947. 9p plus 33 pl Stockholm, 1947.

*175a TÉRIADE, E. Propos de Pierre Bonnard. Verve
5no17-18:[59] Ag 1947.

*176 TERRASSE, CHARLES. Bonnard. 144il (13col) 206p
Paris, Henri Floury, éditeur, 1927.
  Bibliography; list of illustrated work; catalog of
  graphic work by Jean Floury, p187-99.

*176a ——— [Introduction] Verve 5no17-18:[1,3] Ag 1947.

*177 ——— Maisons de campagne de Bonnard. 9il (1col)
Formes et Couleurs 6no2:27-38 1944.

*178 ——— Pierre Bonnard. 2il Le Point no3:93-5
1937.

  Special number "Les maîtres de L'art indépendant 1895-1925. Portraits d'artistes."
  ——— See also bibl 141, 146.

*179 THÉOTE, DANIEL. Pierre Bonnard. 8il Tricolor
1no1:79-90 Ap 1944.
  THIEME-BECKER. See bibl 78.

*180 THOMAS, LOUIS. 120 peintres, sculpteurs, graveurs,
architects, décorateurs. p38-9 Paris, Aux Armes de
France, 1944.

*181 THOME, J. R. Pierre Bonnard (1867-1947). 8il
Le Livre et ses Amis 3no17:9-17 Mr 1947.

182 VAUXCELLES, LOUIS. Pierre Bonnard. 14il(1col,por)
[16]p incl pl Paris, Laboratoires Chantereau, n.d.
  Lettered on cover: Drogues et peintures, album
  d'art contemporain. No.40. Parvillée, éditeur.

182a ——— Pierre Bonnard. 1il Le Carnet des Artistes
no3:12 Mr 1 1917.

183 VERKADE, DOM WILLIBROD. O.S.B. Yesterdays of
an artist-monk. p72-3 London, Burns Oates &
Washbourne, ltd., 1930.
  Translated from the German by John L. Stod-
  dard. Another translation from the original
  Dutch, published as *Le tourment de Dieu, étapes
  d'une moine peintre.* Paris, Rouart et Watelin,
  1923.

*184 VERVE. Couleur de Bonnard. [86]p incl il (some
col) Paris, 1947.
  Special Bonnard issue, v5no17-18 Ag 1947, with
  contributions by Lamotte, Tériade, Terrasse
  (bibl 100a,175a,176a).

  ——— See also bibl 28.

*185 VINDING, NANA. Et brev om Bonnard. 4il (por)
Klingen p83-4 1942.

*186 VOLAVKA, VOJTECH. Fancowszke malirstvi v Prazske
moderní galerii. Zvlástni otisk ze sborniku
"Umeni" 1il p62-4 Praha, Jan Stenc, 1935.

*187 VOLLARD, AMBROISE. Mes portraits. 1il Arts et
Métiers Graphiques no64:39-44 S 15 1938.
  English translation inserted.

*188 ——— Recollections of a picture dealer. 1il p248-54
et passim Boston, Little Brown and co., 1936.
  Translated from the original French manuscript
  by Violet M. MacDonald, subsequently published with some revisions, as *Souvenirs d'un
  marchand de tableaux* Paris, Albin Michel, 1937.

*189 WALDMANN, EMIL. Die Kunst des Realismus und
des Impressionismus im 19. Jahrhundert. p94,123,
149,152 Berlin, Propyläen-Verlag, 1927.

190 WALLIS, ANNE ARMSTRONG. The symbolist painters
of 1890. 1il Marsyas 1:132 1941.

*191 WERTH, LÉON. Bonnard. 2.éd. 81il 52p plus pl

Paris, Editions Georges Crès et cie., 1923. (Cahiers d'Aujourd'hui).
First edition, 1919. Edited by George Besson.

192 ——— Bonnard. Cahiers d'Aujourd'hui no10:191-2 1922.

*193 ——— Bonnard. 5il L'Art Vivant 1no9:1-3 My 1 1925.
Partly reprinted in Bulletin de la Vie Artistique 6no10:217-18 My 15 1925.

194 ——— Eloge de Pierre Bonnard, orné de dix lithographies. [25]p incl pl [Paris?] Manuel Bruker, éditeur, 1947?

*195 ——— La peinture et la mode, quarante ans après Cézanne. 4il p127-33. Paris, Editions Bernard Grasset, 1945.

*196 ——— Quelques peintres. 1il p107-16 Paris, Editions G. Crès, 1923.

——— See also bibl 144.

*197 WILDENSTEIN AND CO., INC., NEW YORK. Exhibition of paintings by Bonnard, March first to twenty-fourth 1934. 15p plus 16pl New York, 1934.
Text consists of commentary by Roger-Marx, Geffroy, Mirbeau, Werth, Fosca, Allard, dated 1894-1924. Biography by Bazin, from L'Amour de l'Art Ap 1933.

*198 WILENSKI, REGINALD HOWARD. The breakfast room. 1il(col) In his: Vanity Fair's portfolio of modern French art. New York, Vanity Fair, 1935.
Text facing color plate 20.

*199 ——— Modern French painters. p141-2,154-6,162 et passim New York, Reynal & Hitchcock, 1940.

*200 WRIGHT, WILLARD HUNTINGTON. Modern painting, its tendency and meaning. 1il p3,5-18 New York and London, John Lane, 1915.

*201 ZERVOS, CHRISTIAN. Pierre Bonnard est-il un grand peintre? 5il (2col) Cahiers d'Art 22:1-6 1947.

ILLUSTRATED BOOKS

TERRASSE, CLAUDE. Petit solfège illustré. Paris, Imprimeries Réunies, 1893. Lithographs in color and black and white.

——— Petits scènes familières pour piano. Paris, Fromont, 1893. 19 lithographs and cover.

MELLERIO, ANDRÉ. La lithographie originale en couleurs. Paris, L'Estampe et l'Affiche, 1898. 2 lithographs (cover and frontispiece).

NANSEN, PETER. Marie. Paris, La Revue Blanche, 1898. 19 brush and ink drawings (line cuts).

VERLAINE, PAUL. Parallèlement. Paris, Ambroise Vollard, 1900. 9 wood engravings, 109 lithographs printed in rose and blue.

JARRY, ALFRED. Grand almanach du père Ubu. Paris, Ambroise Vollard, 1901.

LONGUS. Les pastorales, ou Daphnis et Chloé. Paris, Ambroise Vollard, 1902. 160 lithographs.

RENARD, JULES. Histoires naturelles. Paris, Ernest Flammarion, 1908. 67 brush and ink drawings (line cuts).

MIRBEAU, OCTAVE. La 628-E-8. Paris, E. Fasquelle, 1908. Brush drawings (line cuts).

BARRUCAND, V. D'un pays plus beau. Algiers, L'Akbar & Paris, H. Floury, 1910. 7 drawings (line cuts?).

LA FONTAINE. Fables. n.d.[191?]
"Exemplaire unique sur papier de Chine, avec 144 dessins originaux dans les marges."

GIDE, ANDRÉ. Le Prométhée mal enchaîné. Paris, Nouvelle Revue Française, 1920. 30 drawings (line cuts?).

ANET, CLAUDE. Notes sur l'amour. Paris, Crès, 1922. 14 drawings (engraved on wood by Yvonne Malliez).

CHAVEAU, LÉOPOLD. Histoire du poisson scie et du poisson marteau. Paris, Payot, 1923. 38 drawings (line cuts?).

MIRBEAU, OCTAVE. Dingo. Paris, Ambroise Vollard, 1924. 55 etchings.

CHAVEAU, LÉOPOLD. Histoires du petit Renaud. Paris, Nouvelle Revue Française, 1927. 49 drawings (line cuts with color added by stencil).

ROGER-MARX, CLAUDE. Simili. Paris, Au Sans Pareil, 1930. 7 etchings.

VOLLARD, AMBROISE. La vie de Sainte Monique. Paris, Ambroise Vollard, 1930. 29 drawings (transferred on stone), 17 etchings and 178 compositions (drawn on wood by the artist).

BONNARD, PIERRE. Correspondances. Paris, Verve (Tériade), 1944. Drawings. Early letters illustrated with 28 reproductions of pen, ink or pencil drawings made especially for this publication.

LOUYS, PIERRE. Le crépuscule des nymphes. Paris, Pierre Tisné, 1946. 24 lithographs.

COLETTE. Belles saisons. Paris, Club des Lecteurs de la Gazette des Lettres, 1947. Drawings (line cuts?).

VERVE. Couleur de Bonnard. Paris, Verve (Tériade), 1947. Special issue, Aug 1947. Cover, frontispiece (in color), and all decorations designed by the artist in 1946.

Photograph Credits

Fifteen thousand copies of this book have been printed in March, 1948, for the Trustees of the Museum of Modern Art by The John B. Watkins Company, New York.